BEFORE YOU QUIT WRITING, READ THIS!

Before You Quit Writing, Read This!

23 Stories & Strategies to Keep You Writing

Dave Ursillo Jr.
and *The Literati Writers*

LEAD WITHOUT FOLLOWERS, LLC.

Dave Ursillo Jr.
www.daveursillo.com

The Literati Writers ℠
www.literatiwriters.com

First Edition: July 2013.

ISBN: 1490552979
ISBN-13: 978-1490552972

Also on Amazon Kindle
ASIN: B00DSA53D8

10 9 8 7 6 5 4 3 2 1
BISAC: Art / Individual Artists / Artists' Books

Editing by Stephanie Auteri
Editing and Layout by Cate Spaulding
Cover Artwork and Design by Mars Dorian

Printed in the United States of America

Dedicated to you—
Keep writing.

"The only real advice you can give anyone is to keep writing."

— DAVID SEDARIS

ACKNOWLEDGMENTS

I would like to extend my deepest and most sincere gratitude to the contributing authors of this book, Megan Atkinson, Joe Choi, Jeanine Nicole Cerundolo, Cassia Cogger, Lauryn Doll, Sang Thi Duong, Jessica Glendinning, Joshua Harbert, Clare Herbert, Stephanie Jiroch, Lisa Landtroop, Lori Mancini, Milo McLaughlin, Tom Meitner, Amy Ouellette, Diane Pauley, Jean Powell, Jennifer Price, Kadena Tate, Rona Thau, Caitlin Walsh, Meagan Christine Williams, and Jason Vanfosson. Without you, this book would not be possible. And, I wish to thank you for filling my life with deeper meaning, presence, and joy as members of *The Literati Writers*℠. Working with you has been an honor and pleasure, and I feel blessed to call you each a friend.

Thank you for allowing me to include your beautiful words in this humble work that hopes to keep fellow writers of the world writing. Your words are what make this book unique, and to me they also represent an authentic example of the high ideal to harness our humble lives, stories, struggles and aspirations to help one another find more joy, purpose and fulfillment in creativity, work and love.

Special thanks are further owed to a handful of my loyal

supporters who I enlisted to help assist me with the publication of this book, especially Cate Spaulding, Stephanie Auteri and Mars Dorian. Thank you for all your hard work and dedication in making this book possible.

Finally, to you, the reader, thank you for endeavoring upon this path of writing, creativity and artistry that you have chosen. I consider writing to be a divine art and no matter your experience, comfort level, or relationship to the craft of writing, I sincerely hope that this book helps you feel more deeply understood, empowered and connected to fellow writers of the world who, like you, wish to embrace the curious art of writing to better themselves, to better the quality of their lives, and to better the world around them.

When you next sit down to write, please remember: your words do matter, and our world truly needs them.

CONTENTS

BEFORE YOU QUIT WRITING, READ THIS!

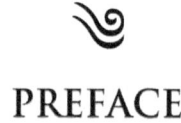

PREFACE

Before You Quit Writing, Read This! exists to keep you writing. This book is a collection of 23 stories and strategies from writers around the world just like you. The authors of this book highly value the idea that, as writers, the creative journey is one of life's greatest rewards. As writers, we must aspire to feel the artistry, depth, nuance, meaning, and beauty throughout every portion of our personal journeys. This book is a testament to that noble value.

The pages of this book give you authentic advice and earnest stories through which you will feel connected to fellow writers, compassionate to the journey we all share with one another, and determined to make your journey the reward. These authors' stories span tales of struggle and overcoming, love and fear, confusion and perseverance, joy and lifelong fulfillment. Beyond all else, *Before You Quit Writing, Read This!* is a resource of motivation and personal inspiration that you can open at any instance of your creative journey when you hear that voice in the back of your head that tells you, "Quit. Quit now."

This book exists because that voice is a liar. And that voice is telling you to quit only because you are scared. I should know. As a writer, I am scared every day. It's not that I find myself trembling in fear for what I have to say, or that you might visit me to find me cowering in a corner after an anonymous critic has left a negative review on Amazon. Having been a writer for 10 years (and working for myself as a writer for over four), in addition to having published two books and having been published in five more, I am still afraid every day for what I write and how it will be received. I wonder if it makes any sense to anyone else besides me. I fear that I am crazy for saying what I feel called to say. I feel perpetually uncertain about where all of this writing and creating is leading me—or if I'm falling behind the pace of everyone else around me. I feel unsure every day about where all the words are even coming from. The creative journey is bound by our fear—because the journey of life is a never-ending confrontation with our fear.

The authors of this book know that feeling, too. This book is a collection of their words: more than 20 honest stories that share advice and strategies from their experiences as writers, artists, and creatives of various ages and levels of experience. In *Before You Quit Writing, Read This!*, these authors have but one message to share with you: "Friend, please do not quit."

They know what it's like to face down their fears and be tempted to quit the writing game altogether. It's because we all, as writers, must face ourselves and our truth from what we create and share. We cannot write for writing's sake, but must endure a long battle with our own fear. Even though we as human beings don't like to admit that we're afraid. We don't like to admit it to strangers on the street, let alone to friends and family or lovers who care deeply for us. Hell, we don't even like to admit it to ourselves. So we throw out 100 excuses, some more valid than others, and we chew over countless more reasons and circumstances and other rationales in an attempt to validate, quantify, and qualify all of our natural fears and worries.

Your fear tells you you're not good enough, when you know in your heart of hearts that you damn well are. Your fear tells you your writing will never get any better, when you know that your growth as a writer is your own choice, a matter of making the time and space to commit to writing more and to getting better and to keep pushing the boundaries of your own (often self-imposed) creative limitations.

The fear says to you that no one is reading your words, and it claims no one ever will. But in the back of your mind, you say, "Perhaps they're not reading because I'm not sharing, or not sharing enough, or not sharing enough of the truth that's etched in my soul and dying to be unleashed."

You tell yourself that your writing skills are not what they could be (but couldn't we say that of so many things, like our health?). You tell yourself that there are a million writers who are better than you, and that they're the ones with all the readers, all the clients, all the blog subscribers (I've never heard of a world that's run out of readers; there are always more than enough to go around).

Maybe you just become so frustrated every time you put pen to paper that you feel emotionally crippled at the sight of a blank page—and instead of fighting the resistance, you acquiesce to the creative struggle and walk away.

Before You Quit Writing, Read This! exists because we are all experiencing these same battles, friend. It's because we're scared. We're unsure. And the path before us is uncertain. You're probably feeling a bit alone in your journey—a curious, unsure adventure that's calling you forth, but which is riddled with so many question marks. But this journey brings with it the promise of a better, healthier, happier life, full of love and joy. You just don't know how to get there—let alone where it might lead once you start walking toward it.

In the face of these natural trials that every human being—especially the writers and creatives among us—must face comes this book, *Before You Quit Writing, Read This!* This book is the embodiment of truth overcoming fear and strength overriding vulnerability. *Before You Quit Writing, Read This!* is the bible upon your nightstand and the coaster under your mug of morning coffee. It is an invocation to keep writing every single day and night, in spite of your doubts, your worries, the circumstances, and every ounce of adversity you'll ever face. This book exists to keep you writing, motivated, and determined to live and love your creative journey, every step of the way.

Before You Quit Writing, Read This! hopes to inspire you by showing you the depths of the most raw and real love (and grit) that have kept the authors of this book writing. This book is a unique collection of 23 original stories that feature real-world advice from writers who are just like you. While you could ordinarily turn to any variety of resources from experts, pop culture icons, and creative geniuses like Stephen King (*On Writing*) or Steven Pressfield (*The War of Art*), this book wishes to indulge your natural humanity and thus your similarity to who could be called an "ordinary in stature" group of authors who hail from several continents and span more than four decades in age. I call this group *The Literati Writers*℠.

As a creative entrepreneur and multi-published author, I felt called to found an online writing community in 2012 with one vital mission in mind: to provide a positive, healthy, and supportive environment for writers of all levels where they could unite to create, converse, and encourage one another to make their creatives journeys all the more rewarding. What resulted was something truly special: a tight-knit, highly positive, and encouraging community of more than 50 men and women who hail from seven countries. *The Literati Writers*℠ are the authors of this book.

In this private online space that fosters genuine friendships, working relationships, and collaboration and publication opportunities, members of *The Literati Writers*℠ learn and grow under my guidance and through their own artistic ingenuity, entrepreneurial explorations, and sheer determination. We share ideas with one another in a private discussion forum. We collaborate on projects like this book in your hands. We participate in live author interviews every month, and each member participates in these calls, asking questions of our interviewees live on the line. I also provide personal support, one-on-one with every member, and share advice, strategies, ideas, and experiences from my more than four years working for myself as a self-employed writer, speaker, multi-published author, and creative entrepreneur.

Thus, the authors of this book span freelance copywriters to five-time authors, young bloggers and "I don't know what I'm doing with my life" journal-keepers, homemakers to college students, hobbyists to budding entrepreneurs. What has brought these authors together in our private community is the exact cause that unites them as authors of this book: on behalf of writers everywhere and in the face of the most fundamental and pervasive creative roadblocks that discourage and derail so many creative men and women, they want to encourage you to shed your fear and awaken to your highest, truest, and most full self.

Those creative roadblocks are manifestations of our fear and worry, and they take the shape of avoidance, creative anxiety, resistance, writers' block, and paralyzing self-doubt. At their root, these creative roadblocks are embodiments of one fear: the fear of our being seen and being judged, of failing, and even of succeeding.

I am thrilled to say that *The Literati Writers*ˢᴹ is a flourishing example that the "tortured writer routine" and the "starving artist routine" are indeed myths reinforced by our fears that we're not good enough, not smart enough, and that we're all alone in our earnest desires to live our journeys in alignment with our values, beliefs, and dreams. This book is a testament to that. I am so proud to put this book in your hands. Each chapter is a unique contribution that has been written with one question in mind: "What would I say to a writer like me who is about to quit writing, in order to keep them writing?"

This book is split into three distinct sections that represent separate stages of every writer's common journey. The first stage speaks to The Emerging Writer, who is fighting a battle of self-belief. The second stage speaks to The Committing Writer, who is deepening her commitment to writing with professionalism by writing *for* others—not just for herself. The third and final stage speaks to The Flourishing Writer, who is striving to make writing a religious vocation and an artful journey that complements her life from top to bottom.

In these pages, you will discover how Stephanie Jiroch never felt comfortable calling herself a writer until the unexpected passing of her mother. You will feel how "good words" saved Diane Pauley from a childhood of negative words that showered her in doubt and insecurity. You will read how Megan Atkinson kept writing when no one was reading, and how Lori Mancini discovered inspiration to write in the heavy breath of her napping dog, Moses. And, you'll be challenged to become a better writer, too. Joshua Herbert reminds you that you don't need reasons to keep writing when you remember that you always have permission to quit. Jean Powell says that writing is a mirror that reflects back to us the truly beautiful selves that lie beneath our skin. And Jennifer Price shares how writing reveals the miracles in life all around her, while Tom Meitner tells you how writing is the last great form of self-expression.

These pages mean to encourage you to open up and go deeper to share your truth, heart, and dreams through writing. The authors of *Before You Quit Writing, Read This!* have united around the love of the written word and the mission to help writers like you live and love your own creative journey just as they do. My hope is that this book provides you with that inspiration, motivation, and keeps you moving forward upon your creative path: in the ink you spread, in the energy you share, and in the kind smiles you offer to passing strangers upon the street.

Please, keep writing, friend.

Dave Ursillo
July 2013

An Invocation to You, Writer on The Brink

By Jeanine Nicole Cerundolo

Dear writer,
Before you quit writing,
Don't.
Instead, remember why it is your birthright.
Remember why you started, one day, once upon a time.
Remember what compelled you to express the words that are
your song.

Dearest writer—
Put away your staff of fire.
Destruction has its proper place.
But today, you are birthing something grand, and generous.

Let the currents of thought pour through you, the vessel.
It is not hard work, it is not effort.
If you struggle, back away.
If you are forcing it, take time to hibernate instead.
Listening is part of writing.
Living your life is part of writing.
Noticing, without touching pen to a single page,
is part of writing.

Dear writer-in-the-making,

I know that it is a hard road sometimes.
I know that it seems like each utterance is frivolous, or selfish.
I know it can feel like pulling teeth to find that flow.
But, writing is the way we know the world;
It is the way we know ourselves.
When you weave your words like that, you touch my heart.
When you sing your song like that, you melt my being.
When you get out of your own way
So that what needs to be said can be said,
You are doing a great service.

You write to release a ribbon of truth and beauty
That did not know itself
'Til you gave it form.

You uncover worlds within you
That were stewing uncontrollably:
Desiring to be manifested, and heard.
The clogged pores of your soul begin to open
When you release thoughts, and expand their being.

Let writing grace you with its presence.
Do not ask for it; it will ask for you.
Listen to the way your name sounds on its tongue.
How much it loves you.

One day, all the words fell silent.
One day, all the canvases were blank.
One day, you sat cradling your head in your hands,
And you wanted to throw in the towel.

Wrap yourself in it instead.
Let it warm you, sink into the embrace of loneliness.

Be still for a while.
Then, when the quiet has had its turn,
It will surrender, like all things do.

Just as the dusk becomes the dawn,
So too do you cycle through phases of pauses, and growth.
Not just once crossing this threshold,
But, every night, transforming, over and over.

I want to hear what you have to say.
Do you write for your own expression? Or do you begin with me
in mind? Picturing my adoring gaze upon your scrawlings?
Consolidate history in your sentences.
Etch a future that you can dare create.

And then, when the judge comes to the table
With his gavel and beady scorning eyes,
Just smile at him.

He wants to protect you, in the end.
He wants to make your offering the best that it can be.
He wants to save you from the scorn that may befall exposure.
But, his seat is only warmed for so long.

When he has worn out his welcome,
Sit him in a corner facing the wall,
And let the children play.
They streak streams of color on the white walls,
And throw their heads back with peals of delightful, delighted
laughter.

You are the prisoner dressed in black.
You are the goddess bedecked in rose petals.

You are the chalice offering eternal life.
You are the wilting leaf on a hot day.

Your salvation lies here, in the way you whisper to the page.
The page who understands you and promises never to forget.
The page who knows you better than anyone:
Better than your lover, better than God, better than yourself.
(well, maybe not better than God).
He listens when you write, and it pleases Him.
She softens at the touch of your transformation
And it eases Her.

Become ashes today when you author your own story.
Become the phoenix who abandons itself recklessly to the flame.
Do not resist. Do not struggle.
Simply, surrender.
Writing happens to you and through you.
Writing courses through your veins.

Writing pulses in your heart,
the one that I can see now.

The one that I offer,
here to you.

Jeanine Nicole Cerundolo is a writer, certified yoga instructor, and trained group coaching facilitator who facilitates transformation in people's lives. Through her experience with social work and education, coupled with a passion for global activism and community service, she believes that much lasting change in our world begins from the inside out. She is passionate about poetry, creative expression, aligning her activities with her interests, and helping others to similarly follow their bliss. Jeanine is currently exploring life's exciting terrain through her blog, ZestForTheQuest.com.

PART ONE

The Emerging Writer

THE EMERGING WRITER

By Dave Ursillo

It always begins by emerging: every journey, every effort, every moment in which a human soul stands upon his or her feet for the first time with vigor and determination. Emergence is a birth. It is a rebirth. It comes after decades of lying in wait, quietly and impatiently, before the seed of your soul finally bursts through the surface. It comes by chance in a moment of dawning understanding: a sudden, brilliant epiphany that awakens an unconscious yearning that had lain dormant within your spirit forever—perhaps for lifetimes.

Every journey first begins by emerging. And for the writer, there is a long road from emergence to flourishing. That is because the road first starts—as it does for every soul, whether writer or not—from a place of timidity and fear. Emerging can only happen by crawling out into the sun from a protected, rocky enclave of doubt. And what keeps us in the shadows where every worried soul lurks (some for decades upon end) is a bright white wall named Fear. We see with our swollen pupils that bright white wall and think that it will scathe and burn us for, already, just by looking upon it, the wall singes our sight—it makes us squint hard, frown, and turn away.

But the bright white wall named Fear is a barrier of deceit, for we know that the light is nourishing: it is life, it is promise, it is warmth. The sunshine holds the promise of what could be, and all that may lay beyond the quiet, dark, safe, familiar enclave. The light draws us to it. We wish to reach our hands into it, even if it might burn us. We wish to look upon the sun above, even if it sears our sight.

The sun, the light, they are all a promise of what could be. For the writer who lies in wait, there is no greater temptation than what could be—for "what could be" is the purest exemplification of the writer's greatest and most powerful asset: raw, human imagination.

WHO IS THE EMERGING WRITER?

The Emerging Writer is writing to stand up and stand out. It is the most important goal, the single most important feat that you as an emerging writer can commit to, over and over again.

Write. Stand up. Stand out.

But who, exactly, is the Emerging Writer? She says she is still an "aspiring" this or a "someday" that. He places a disclaimer around every description of what he wishes, dreams of, and desires. Her grandest, most earnest wishes for her life are also her deepest, darkest secrets. He wants to be a writer, but is afraid that he is simply not "enough" of one. The Emerging Writer is locked in a quiet confrontation. Nameless and noiseless as that confrontation might be, the conflict is not without struggle or repercussion—for the confrontation she faces is with herself.

The Emerging Writer is facing her own truth: the soul beyond the face and identity and stories of herself that reflect back in her mind's mirror.

Writing has called to her on a profound level. Invisible, intangible, and outright indescribable, her calling to write represents a curious, mysterious intrigue—the only answer is to write. However, she has a feeling that what she will discover through her words is the truest version of herself she's ever met. Remarkably, discovering, acknowledging, and accepting this truth is a very troubling proposition for her—because she knows that when she sees it for the first time, she'll never be able to forget it again.

The reason? The Emerging Writer is locked in a battle with belief. Belief is the Emerging Writer's battleground: the earliest stage of your writing journey whereupon every battle is one between belief or disbelief, commitment and avoidance, pursuit of the ideal or settling for something less, venturing toward distant dreams or acquiescing before those visages in fear.

Are you an emerging writer? If so, you're probably feeling this battle between belief and disbelief. It's a troubling feeling: a tear that separates your longing heart from your weary mind. One preaches the reckless pursuit of your love, even in the face of your fear; the other reprimands you for "selfishly" thinking you deserve more than anyone else.

And so you find yourself locked in deafening, internal debates and dialogues that make your head spin. You want to believe that your words are worth reading, but you're just not so sure of it. "How can anyone say for sure?" you tell yourself, "and why should my words be any better, or any different, or any more special than anyone else's?" Doubt creeps into your beating heart. "What have I got to say that someone else hasn't already said—someone who's probably smarter, and more popular, and more educated, and more respected? Someone who has more fame, more acclaim, more power, more status, and more wealth than me?"

Your fear tells you that these rationalizations make you unworthy of what you want. Your fear tells you that you're undeserving of your most earnest, honest, and humble of desires.

Writing is how you begin to will your unrelenting heart over your weary mind. Through the written word, you begin to shape your intangible beliefs into physical existence: you court your so-called "flippant" emotions and thoughts, and feelings, your instincts and intuition, your values and beliefs into life. Into form! Writing is birthing your belief into reality. And it is why the practice of writing is so important to the Emerging Writer: the soul who is longing to believe.

Emerging is a confrontation with belief. And for every writer, artist, or creative who has ever lived and will ever live, believing in yourself is not just a requirement: it's a religion. The religion is faith in love; in endless and raw human potential; in the capabilities we all possess not only as writers but as human beings to equally channel divinity, or universal truth, or cosmic energy, or unabashed love, in our lives. The writer embraces just one form of that manifestation: through the pen, and through words.

When you're an emerging writer, you needn't concern yourself with writing the next great novel trilogy or a sprawling manifesto that will live on through the annals of history. Your noble mission is simple: to forge a deeper, stronger understanding of yourself and your humble place in this grand world, amongst all its people. When you emerge, you're challenging yourself to believe. You want to believe that you're more than capable of writing a great story, or sharing an important life lesson, or harnessing the quiet power of the written word in order to generate bigger change in some way, shape, or form. And that all begins through simple, earnest writing, through which you find greater understanding and awareness of yourself. Every stroke of the pen is a deepening practice in your own self-belief.

The Emerging Writer is writing to stand up and stand out. But emerging isn't only about being seen: it's about you facing down your own fears, doubts, and disbelief, as well as the remarkable discomfort that dawns from being seen by others, judged by wary or cynical eyes, and criticized by dissenters. It's even about overcoming the seductive allure of praise by new fans and believers.

Just remember: The Emerging Writer often forgets that her grandest mission is not to help others believe in themselves, or even to help others believe in her own self. The mission is to stand up, stand out, and shine—because before you can prove anything to anyone, you need to prove it to yourself.

As an emerging writer, the hard truth is this: even you don't yet fully believe in yourself.

It's your own writing that will turn you into a believer.

YOU'RE ALREADY
A 'GOOD ENOUGH' WRITER

By Joe Choi

It was a shitty situation. Literally.

I had no idea what to do. I stood in front of the clogged toilet, wondering if I should tell my host family or just leave it for the next person to deal with. If I told the host family, I could say it wasn't me. It was whoever used the bathroom before me. I'd be off the hook.

But sometimes the messenger gets shot and killed. If I left it for the next person, I could get blamed for it, and then I'd get in trouble, despite my pleas of, "It wasn't me. I swear!"

We were a group of teenagers staying with a Russian host family while we were away at hockey camp. Victor, the dad, spoke broken English with a very thick accent. But when he got angry, you knew it. He had no trouble keeping a bunch of punk teenagers in line. That's why I was shakin' in my drawers at the prospect of reporting the unfortunate news of the clogged toilet.

Isn't it funny how that works?

Even though Victor had limited English vocabulary and mispronounced words all the time, he could still get his message across. But it wasn't just about anger and instilling fear in people. He could be happy and fill a room with laughter and joy. He could tell a story about growing up in the Soviet Union and bring a tear to your eyes. He could tell his story about immigrating to

North America and fill you with inspiration and hope.

Some of his stories made me giggle because of his accent and mispronunciations. Like the story about the time he "went to the beach." An outsider, or anybody joining mid-story, would be very confused. After all, the bitch was very beautiful.

But it wasn't really about the words he was using. It was the intention behind those limited words that made the difference. Plenty of people are more skilled with words than Victor. But they lack intention, so they end up putting their audience to sleep.

I don't have a way with words either. But I find comfort in Victor's abilities. Because, despite my limitations, I somehow make money from writing. When I had to read Shakespeare and Poe in school, I used CliffsNotes because I couldn't understand the books. (Or maybe I was just lazy. Who knows.) I still don't know what a lot of vocabulary words mean, and I'm still unsure of a lot of the grammar rules (this despite taking English composition in college). I don't even think I know how to properly use a semicolon.

A lot of the writing pieces in this book you're holding now will probably be way over my head. I don't have a lot in my toolbox. But that's okay. No matter where you think your writing skills are, there's a place for your words. Simple words and simple writing can move the masses.

Simplicity is an art, as is complexity. All writing is art, from that large billboard on the highway with only three words to the great American novel with over 50,000 words and an elaborate plotline.

Some of the greatest songs in history use only three chords, the same chords a complete beginning musician would learn. But it's the intention behind the chords that makes the songs powerful. Three simple chords can move the masses.

Whatever you have in your writer's toolbox at this moment

can move the masses. Don't worry about being an imposter. I've been an imposter many times in my life. So if I end up being an imposter with writing, I could just add it to this list:

- I once lied in a job interview and said I had a 3.0 GPA when I only had a 2.934. And I told them I was interested in their company and the industry. I wasn't. I still got hired.

- When I got to college, I told "the guys" that I'd had sex with lots of girls in high school so I'd seem cooler. That number was actually zero.

- I lied about my income once so I could go to a timeshare sales presentation and get a $100 prize. I had no income, was broke, and needed that $100. The timeshare salesman kept telling me how stupid I was for not taking advantage of the timeshare deal he was offering me. If only he knew the entire story.

- While on dates, I told girls that I had a job and was stable, because that's what I thought they wanted to hear. But there was nothing but pure fucking chaos and uncertainty behind the scenes. I just needed someone to lean on.

- I once agreed with a girl and said I didn't like George W. Bush because I wanted her to like me. But I have nothing against George W. Bush. He seems like a pretty cool guy and I enjoyed his biography. Why couldn't I just be honest and say that?

But with writing, I never feel the need to try to pretend. What I can offer right now is good enough for somebody, somewhere. And a year from now, it'll be good enough for a different somebody, somewhere.

What you have to offer is already good enough for somebody, somewhere.

When I write, my thoughts and feelings are taken down just as they are—raw, real, and untouched by outside toxins. That's exactly how you should strive to keep yours. Because when you take your toolbox and your raw thoughts and feelings, your intention pierces through each page you write, and becomes loud and clear.

There are no imposters. Only scared people. Everyone is scared. The blogger is afraid to hit publish because she's afraid of what people might think. The copywriter is afraid that his latest promotion won't win over prospects. The author is afraid that the latest book won't be as good as the last.

When you write, you give away something that's hard to give away. For that, you deserve all the credit in the world.

So before you hang 'em up, please keep these thoughts with you.

I ended up telling my host family about the clogged toilet and things turned out okay.

They always do.

Joe Choi is a direct response copywriter for the health market. He usually tries something completely new every two years just to shake things up. Through all these shake-ups, his addiction to golf, yoga, avocados, tuna cooked rare, donuts, and beef jerky have remained the same. You can find him at his local golf course or yoga studio, or writing about a bunch of things at FescueFairways.com. Follow him on Twitter @jchoi007.

WRITING WHEN NO ONE IS LOOKING

By Megan Atkinson

As a writer, part of the thrill of the journey is sharing my work. Getting my words into other people's hands and seeing or hearing how it connected with their experience is a succulent, overwhelmingly delightful thrill. We writers thrive on it. Well, most of us do.

But what happens when our work isn't making it to the eyes and hands of eager readers? What happens when our work just isn't getting the exposure and the attention it deserves?

We get hard on ourselves.

We tell ourselves it's not good enough to make that connection with other people. We proclaim that our efforts as writers are pointless. And we try to tell ourselves we should quit: quit trying, quit working so hard at it, or quit writing altogether.

I've been there more times than I can count. I've cried over hundreds of pages of loose-leaf heart and soul that never seemed to make its way out into the world of "real" writers. I've thrown out more journals than I care to admit. I've thrown in the towel over and over and over again.

But the words kept pulling me back.

Some years ago, I surrendered to the quitting. Working full-time, going to school full-time, and trying to manage a personal life made it easy to abandon the words. There wasn't time. I didn't have the energy. Exams were just around the corner.

Deadlines were hovering.

I hadn't scribbled a word beyond a few sticky note reminders and the monthly rent check in years. I said to hell with being a writer and I resolved to make art in some different fashion. I was completely content with leaving that part of my life behind... until my brother died.

We all knew it was coming. He'd been sick for nearly a decade. I knew the day would come when he wouldn't be able to fight anymore. I thought I had prepared myself for what was sure to happen eventually. But I wasn't at all ready for him to take a piece of me with him when he left.

I didn't know what to do with myself. I was distraught and confused. I felt blindsided by something I'd known would happen for years. I went through the phases of grieving but I just didn't feel the same. The sun didn't seem to shine as it used to. The air didn't smell as I remembered it. The hours passed at a slower pace while, inexplicably, days flew by faster.

Things felt broken and foreign and I felt powerless to the grief.

I went to counselors. I saw my doctor. I tried medication to help me stop weeping at any and everything that reminded me of my big brother. Nothing seemed to help. After so many failed attempts at fixing whatever was so broken inside of me, I remembered what had always made me feel whole in years past.

I remembered I was once a writer.

I picked up my pen again and bought some new journals. I wrote letters to my brother when the thought of never hearing his voice again became too overwhelming. When I didn't know how to process what was going on inside my head and within my heart, I wrote until my wrists burned. I wrote until I could make sense of things again.

Not a single other soul on this earth has read those journals. I've never shared them with my family or even my closest friends. They've never been posted to a blog or seen by another set of eyes. I wrote strictly for myself. For the first time ever, I intentionally wrote while absolutely no one else was looking, and it changed my life forever.

I wrote my way out of a gray and dreary world ruled by grief and heartache. I forged a path through the pain. I scratched and clawed with every word I had to beat what had been holding me down. Once I had managed to make it to the other side of awful, the words didn't stop. They had much bigger plans for me.

Once I became confident in the powerful relationship I had created with these words of mine… once I realized just how influential a few adjectives, a handful of choice verbs, and a whole lot of exclamation points could become… the words and I started a whole new adventure.

First, it started with a blog. I had so many ideas and opinions. I had knowledge that needed to be shared with others. So I shared it. The blog was never hugely successful and it never made me a dime, but it was mine. It was my special place for the words and the ideas that finally allowed me to connect with other people in a way I never thought I had the credibility to do.

Eventually, my writing fell into the hands of all the right people, the people my story was meant to be shared with. The words finally won: I became a copywriter. By day, I use my words to save the planet, one kilowatt hour at time. After hours, the words use me to inspire the masses, influence change, and infuse more good into the world with nonprofits and social entrepreneurs.

I used to write to impress. Eventually, I wrote to mourn. I wrote to weed through the jungle of emotions I couldn't navigate otherwise.

Now, I write for a living. As a copywriter, I experience the power of my words every single day. I get to visit with my words to earn a living. I get to dance with my words to make a difference in the world. I write to play. I write to celebrate. I write to teach. I write to live. I write because, without my words, I would be lost.

Your words are with you whether you lay claim to being a writer or not. You can say you're going to quit, but the words won't quit on you. The words will find you no matter what. Whether you're writing your best-selling novel or just documenting the recollection of a sweet memory from yesteryear, you are a writer. You will always be a writer and the words will always be with you... whether someone is looking or not.

Megan Atkinson *is the Chief Word Nerd at Ignite Your Cause, where doing good and doing business are not mutually exclusive. She's merged the artistry of the written word with her philanthropic tendencies to help nonprofits and social entrepreneurs inspire the masses, influence change, and infuse more good into the world. When she's not writing for a cause, she works with solopreneurs to devise sizzling give-back action plans that bolster their brands and deliver the warm fuzzies. To infuse a dash of do-goodery into the work you do, visit IgniteYourCause.com.*

WRITERS KNOW:
SANDBOXES AREN'T JUST FOR KIDS

By Caitlin Walsh

When we were kids, there was the sandbox, filled with toys and friends. We'd build things, destroy things, and then start all over. It didn't matter how small it was, or how quickly we could dig to the bottom of the box. We had total power over the sand.

Then, when we reached our 20s, we played computer games, and that sandbox we had as little kids showed up again, this time complete with a monitor and a mouse. It didn't matter if we weren't running the fastest machine out there because, once we put the disc of The Sims or Roller Coaster Tycoon into the CD-ROM drive, we were kings once again. We had total control and could create anything we wanted. A roller coaster that crashed every time? Why not? Two neighbors who hate each other at first and then fall in love and raise a family? All in the span of an hour? Sure.

But those sandboxes have limits and rules. You need a computer to play the game, or the box in which to actually put the sand.

When we put words on paper or, in the modern world, on a screen, the power comes rushing back. But there are no strings attached this time, no rules to play by, and no objective to beat.

We just have pure creation.

At first, there is only darkness. But with four words, "let there be light," we can see each other. Do you see what I did there? I wrote some words and changed the environment.

Writing is creation and change wrapped up in one simple action. By putting words down, an environment is changed. An environment that can be visited again and again both by writer and reader. Our imaginations are linked by the cyclical act of writing and reading. I can envision something and write it down, and you can see it.

Writing is the ultimate sandbox. We carry over what we learned from our previous sandboxes. Instead of Sims to play god with, we create fleshed-out characters with lives of their own. Instead of sandcastles, we build stories. And while we still can find a certain satisfaction in destroying a story, we know it's more enjoyable to share it with others.

But we're not kids anymore, and real life doesn't have the same rules computer games did. Just because we write something doesn't mean we get paid in points or dollars. All that freedom and expression isn't guaranteed to put food on the table.

I got the chance to major in writing. But I found that, after four years of writing classes, I began to lose sight of the sandbox. Each semester, I had to adjust to a new professor with different rules of what was acceptable and what was not. Some assignments were pretty open-ended, while others were quite exact. Sometimes, writing for a grade wasn't fun.

Luckily, I discovered National Novel Writing Month.

"NaNoWriMo," as insiders call it, has as its main goal pure creation. Participants are tasked with writing 50,000 words in 30 days. It doesn't matter how bad those words are because, by December 1, there are 50,000 more words than there were on November 1. This is a competition, but you're not up against the other writers. You're up against yourself for bragging rights. Can you silence your inner editor long enough to reach the goal?

November 2011 was exhilarating. I created with total freedom, something I hadn't felt in a long time. I mostly wrote by the seat of my pants. There wasn't any outlining beforehand. I just set off with an idea and started writing. I was creating again, and this time I didn't have to cater to professors or assignments. Finally, I was writing something that was wholly my own.

I found my sandbox again. And I'm never losing sight of it again.

Caitlin Walsh *was born, raised, and currently lives in Boston, but took a four-year detour to Long Island for college. She dreams of being an author, of selling books in stores, and of earning a living by her printed words. For now, though, she works behind the scenes for a financial news website by day, and by night is usually knee deep in her novel draft or another writing project that she started to avoid her novel. She spends most of her free time on the T, traveling to various meet-ups, groups, and activities. She also lives on the Internet at @WalshCaitlin.*

FIND THE INSPIRATION WITHIN

By Lori Mancini

I was looking for inspiration around my yoga studio on a rainy afternoon. As a TV sports producer, yoga studio owner, and writer, I was trying to get both a TV project and a writing project off the ground. The computer screen stared blankly at me and I felt that wee bit of panic settling in my chest. Some days, there's nothing more frightening than a blank screen. As staring at it was not making anything magically appear, I reached out into cyberspace and did a random sampling of my trusted friends to see what inspired them. I was completely surprised by their answers.

"Helping others and trying to be a better person each day."
"Ice cream. And my lovely family and friends."
"The prayers of my grandmother."
"The voice of my soul."
"Paddling... camping... being outside."

The consensus seemed to be that inspiration could be found in others, and through service for others. I was stunned. I'm not sure what I expected. Maybe more of an internal soul search? I have always believed that the wisdom you seek comes from within. You just have to awaken it. After all, as the poet Rumi wrote, "I looked in temples, churches and mosques. But I found the Divine within my heart."

My friends' responses got me thinking about inspiration as

energy. Which meant that inspiration was everywhere, in everything. We just needed to pay attention and to know what to look for, to see what resonated. We needed to find the flow and go with it, tap into its force and use that momentum to our advantage.

With that in mind, I wandered upstairs to the main yoga studio, computer in hand, with my canine companions Moses and Baku trailing behind. I sat in that calming, airy room and, as I looked around the beautiful space, I realized it was home to thousands of students. It once again dawned on me that they came here to recharge on so many different levels. The thing that made people keep coming back was intangible.

I soaked up the vibe, trying to be still and delve deeper. I heard my breath. I heard Mo's contented sigh. Baku shifted against my leg. Eventually, I started to tap into the collective energy of the studio. Stories hung haphazardly in the air. The past experiences of all the students who had inhabited this room created an energy that still lingered. I stepped into it. Inspiration swirled around me and words flowed effortlessly.

My friends are right: Inspiration can be anywhere and everywhere. You just have to find the energetic source that resonates within you.

What inspires you?

__Lori Mancini__ is a freelance television sports producer, yoga studio owner, and writer. Between her love of Boston sports, yoga, and communication, Lori believes in meeting passion, loyalty, and dedication in all areas of her life. Her yoga studio, Laughing Elephant Yoga, is based in East Greenwich, Rhode Island, and can be found at LaughingElephantYoga.com. When she's not working with major television networks like ESPN and CBS, she can be found biking across New England and walking her white Labrador retriever, Moses.

GOOD WORDS SAVED ME

By Diane Pauley

The simplest of human actions executed with the wrong intention can often be someone's undoing. That was certainly the case for me. My stepmother wanted the love from me that I had for my real mother but, when my mom died, that love suffered a massive heart attack and couldn't be revived. Because of this gap between us that couldn't be bridged, I was verbally abused for the next 15 years. It was during this time that the writer in me died.

My stepmother took the simplest of things—her words—and started to use them to cut me down. As a result, the once starry-eyed lover of words began to loathe writing of any kind.

Before my birth mother Vivian became an angel in the sky, she wrote about lovely things, participating quietly in humanity with her words. I, too, picked up this habit early on and began to have a love affair with literature, writing my own depictions of everything from sails at sea all the way to murder mysteries. I was in love with this subdued but emotionally invested form of powerful expression.

But my stepmother was not Vivian by any means, and that stepmother had no love for the written word. The verbal put-downs began with harmless phrases like, "You're not cleaning it right—you're doing a half-ass job," or, "Don't you care what they think of you—put on something more respectful."

My once proud inward affirmations of love and certainty

began to retreat and wave a white flag. I soon turned outward for validation, associating my worth with shallow banter and respectful exchanges. My writing ceased to be my staple meal because I could no longer afford to write lovely words of value if they weren't considerate of all humanity.

My writing eventually became a shell of what once was, mirroring what was happening inside me. This was a direct result of my stepmother's increasingly aggressive verbal attacks: "Don't cry. Grow up already. Stop manipulating us with your tears," or "Really, who would want you... a selfish, lifeless person like you?"

Every harsh word was like a fresh cut to an already stinging wound. I hurriedly licked them clean, doing all I could to prevent another blow. My writing during these years reflected just that. It was shallow, appeasing, respectful... a downright slap in the face to the good writer I used to be.

Finally, after years of verbal defilement, I took a shovel and dug that damn good writer out of my soul ground where I had buried her. I was so sick and tired of all of the bad words. I wanted truth; I wanted my truth to come out. I wanted to see, hear, write, speak, and be those loving words that were ripped away from me.

Music saved me. Whitman, Emerson, Austen, and Jesus saved me. I held onto every single lovely, angelic, heavenly word like it was my last drop of water and I was near death, having been parched for the last 15 years. I shut out the abuser's wrong words and turned to those who knew me—the real me—and they spoke life over me.

"You're so worth it." "You didn't deserve it." "You're so strong." "Your smile shows off your inner light." "It wasn't your fault."

Thank you. God. Those words felt good.

Distorted images in my mind started to see the light. I began to uncover more and more truth as I wrote. I let the loving words pour over me and wash my shattered inner palette clean.

Devilish became Devoted.
Ill-minded morphed into Innocent.
Angry gave itself over to Angelic.
Naïve blossomed into Nice.
Evil transformed into Enchanting.

I became a whole Diane. The writer in me was found again because she had never left. I merely had to unveil her because she had been hidden under years of grime, dirt, and debris.

The good words saved me.

Diane Pauley *is a writer and life coach who has been writing since she was 6 years old. Diane carried her passion for the written word with her through high school, but abandoned her love of writing in pursuit of a safe, money-making career in law. Diane soon decided her heart wasn't in the traditional life route, so she threw her safe plans out the window. Today, Diane has returned to her roots and is using her passion for people and the written word to coach young post-grads who feel like they've lost their way. Join Diane's mission to rediscover your true identity at PostGradolescence.com.*

THE NEGATIVE SPACE OF 'I AM'

By Jason Vanfosson

Burn it all. Delete every tweet. Unsend every email. I wanted to take back every single thing I ever wrote—from pre-school alphabet practice sheets to my Master's thesis. After years of holding the romantic notion in my head that I would sit down to a 1937 Royal Typewriter with a gin and tonic while a beam of light sent divine inspiration through me, I aborted this thought and realized no writer sits down to a perfect first draft.

I have always loved reading and writing. I used reading as inspiration and escape. Writing also gave me a way to cope with a less-than-stellar childhood. In my writing I sought revenge against the bullies who turned my days into a series of unending night terrors. Writing became the way I communicated with the world. I would prefer to leave notes for my parents instead of speaking to them. I ordered pen pals from all around the world and loved the sensation of writing to someone around the globe and sharing stories. Eventually, I took a creative writing class and started to write creatively and fell in love with writing all over again.

Despite my closeness to the act of writing, I hit a funk where writing became a joyless exercise. Graduate school in literature and criticism sucked my creativity out of my soul and morphed writing from a joy-filled activity to an excruciating chore. Surrounded by creative writers working on their MFAs and doctorates in poetry and fiction, I struggled with the pervasive thought that I was not a writer. Anything I wrote was an embarrassment to my life and to writers all around the globe. I vowed to never put fingers to keyboard or pen to paper again.

Eventually, I wrote through this block with the support of a coach and a writer's group. A therapist and running endorphins also helped. After some time of getting my writing mojo back, I did some serious writer soul-searching. I continued conversations with my writing coach. I continued attempting to write. I popped out a poem. I started a blog. I read books on the craft of writing. I worked on finding my love for writing again.

On a flowerful and sun-shining May day, I reflected on all the times I wanted to call it quits, change direction, and never write again. I remembered the moments I did not want to be a writer, and the moments I doubted I even had the ability to write words into sentences. Maybe I was not meant to be a writer. Even though I knew deep down in the hidden cobweb-filled corners of my soul that writing was my calling, I could never remember actually wanting to be a writer. I could, however, recall at least six million different moments in my life in which I doubted, rejected, and screamed that I was not a writer.

On the day I was thinking back on all of this, I went to a bookstore and had a conversation with a confidant of mine. In the cozy, cushioned chairs that are coveted at bookstores, I had the epiphany: "I keep telling myself 'I am not a writer' or 'I don't know if I am one.' I feel like I'm living in the negative spaces between the I ams." Suddenly, everything made sense.

I had been so focused on doubt, and on defining myself as not. I had become so entrenched in not being a writer that I missed the whole point. I was frustrated that I was not producing any written work. I was pissed that I was not getting published, even though I had never submitted my work to anyone for publication. Then and there, under the fluorescent lights of the bookstore, I murmured, "I'm a writer." The speech was so quiet and meek that the person I confided in gave me a what-the-hell-just-came-out-of-your-mouth look. I cleared my throat of the doubtful residue and assuredly repeated, "I am a writer." I declared it.

Gurus, coaches, and theologians stress the importance of the I-am statement. No one, though, talks much about the I-am statement's sinister sister I-am-not. Even though she is not discussed as much, many people work from that scary place of I-am-not. This is the place that may have led you to pick up this book. These are the mornings when you stare at a blank page and think, "I'd rather be water-boarded by the literary Gods than do this with an AWOL muse." These are the nights when you want to light fire to everything and call it quits on your writing career.

The negative moments between the I AM moments are crevices any writer can fall into. These are traps between all the other I-am statements we easily proclaim. I am a student. I am a friend. I am a son. I am. In the crevices between these statements, we say things like, "I'm not good enough to be a writer." "I am not a writer. Never will be." "I don't even know if I want to be a writer." When I said these things to myself, I questioned my talent, my dedication, and my passion. Questioning is good. It's how we figure out we're on the wrong path. But we also need to take responsibility for our work.

When you deny that you are a writer, you do something amazing. You let yourself off the hook. So what if you fail? You aren't a writer anyway. You don't have to write every day. After all, you are not a real writer. Denying your writing permits you to step away, give up, give in, and never try. If, for example, I say, "I am not a writer," I can accept failure more easily and not take responsibility for my literary life. Saying I am not a writer means not submitting my work to a publisher and not receiving rejection or acceptance letters.

Declaring yourself a writer, though, forces you to put your work into the world and welcome acceptance, rejection, and the spaces in between as part of the process. When we declare ourselves writers, we become accountable to ourselves and to the world. We can't not write, then.

Jason Vanfosson writes fiction and nonfiction. He is a life coach to artists, writers, creatives, and entrepreneurs who want to lead brazen lives of creativity. His alter ego is working on his Ph.D. in American literature at Western Michigan University, where he also teaches composition, introduction to literature, and American literature. You can read his super secret experimental blog and connect with him on social media by visiting JasonVanfosson.com.

I AM NOT A WRITER

by Amy Ouellette

I am not a writer. I have not felt the desire to write for the sake of writing. And yet, writing is something that refuses to be ignored. I am finally starting to accept that if I don't embrace it and learn to cultivate it as a habit, I won't achieve the things I want, nor will I reach the depths inside of me I feel compelled to explore.

There is a small part of me that has always known this. Why else would I return time and time again to journaling? In the past, the journals would only come out when I was experiencing extreme negative emotion. The only thing I could think to do was to put it down on paper. As if pouring words onto paper would drain them from my head, leaving room for quiet.

I've written about mistakes, loss, and feeling lost. I've written pleas for change (or for nothing to change, when I knew I was being left in a relationship). I even wrote an "I quit" letter (it was never delivered, but I know I slept much better that night). I've written letters on three separate occasions (all delivered) when friendships or relationships had ended. On all of these occasions, the only way I knew to process my emotions was to write, whether to myself or to others.

I'd like to start a new pattern, though, in which writing does not only stem from negative emotions but, rather, is used as a tool of self-exploration. I have had such a hard time putting into words the best emotions I've had and the happiest or most fulfilling times I have experienced. I know my biggest heartaches, because I committed these to paper. I want to be able to say that

I know what makes me feel happiness and satisfaction... what makes me feel alive.

While I want journaling to be a way to discover myself, I also want it to be something that, done consistently, will build my writing muscle. Because, eventually, I want to translate what I find out about myself into something tangible I can offer to the world.

I am a consumer of others' writings, whether through blogs, books, or even song lyrics. I've read books that could take me out of my surroundings into someone else's world. I've read blog posts designed to turn someone's experiences into something from which I could learn. Everyone goes in search of guidance at some point or another.

In my case, I felt overwhelmed by debt when I finished school. I spent days reading all of the blog posts and articles I could find about paying off debt... days consuming what many others had taken the time to put into words—for me. And as I learned from these strangers and had my own experiences of victory over student loans and consumer debt, I started to realize that I wanted to empower others in the same way these writers had empowered me. I wanted to build my ability to write so that I, too, could teach others through my struggles that taking control of your finances is a freeing experience.

So what holds me back? Why am I not a writer? When I start to picture how I can serve others, the picture gets a bit hazy. Sure, I could start a blog. But who am I, and what do I have to say? How long before I run out of topics? Put me in a room with someone and I'll talk their ear off about personal finance tools and strategies (sorry!).

Put me in front of a computer screen, however, and nothing happens.

What I want to happen is for some part of my brain—the

part that has thought through all of these things and can converse about it—to magically spew all of that into perfectly formed sentences that engage the reader and make them instantly grasp that I can teach them something, and that I am worth knowing. I want to skip the part where I flounder, not knowing what to say or how to say it. I want to skip the part where no one is reading what I have to say (though it better be fucking great when someone does read it). It's this fear of being less than perfect when presenting to the world. Logically, I know people start small and learn and grow over time. And I'm not too lazy to do the work. But I let my fear of what others will think if I build in front of them hold me back.

No more. The only way to arrive is to start to move, to take those first steps in some direction, even if that direction changes over time. I need to build the habit: by journaling, by sitting down and putting this knowledge and experience into words, and by hitting that "publish" button. I will try and no one will read it. I will struggle to continue, but I will keep putting words on paper until they make sense. And someday, all of these words will find someone in need, someone looking for guidance, and these words will help them free themselves as well.

My brain tells me I'm not a writer. I'm starting to think that it's a liar.

Amy Ouellette *is a retirement plan consultant, personal finance geek, and aspiring nutritarian. She has been consulting and collecting credentials in the finance industry for almost 10 years, while student loans and other debt allowed her to turn her fear into a hunger for knowledge and action on the personal finance side. Amy's desire to become a better writer is twofold. First, she wants to rediscover journaling in order to explore her values and identity. Then, she wants to focus those values on the task of connecting with and teaching others (perhaps about finance) through stories and inspiration. Find her on Twitter @aeouellette03.*

WRITE TO POWER

by Dave Ursillo Jr.

I believe that we are experiencing a major problem with power in our world today. Turn on the news and you'll hear dozens of political commentators from both sides of the aisle speak nonchalantly of the inability of our modern-day leaders to be effective, efficient, moral and just. Look to sports and Hollywood and the stories we hear revolve around rampant recreational and performance-enhancing drug use. When it comes to our modern day discussions revolving around power and those who have it, the conversation is synonymous with cheating, lying and scandal, corruption and betrayal, weapons charges and spousal abuse and sometimes even death.

Socially and individually, our relationships with power are wildly dysfunctional: from the highest levels of democratic representation permeating down to our neighborhoods and school yards, power has become perverted. And, if you and I share the desire to revolutionize not only what it means to have power but wish to reinforce higher standards of social expectations for those with power, we need to relearn what power means. I believe that redefinition can begin through writing.

If you want to tap into your own unique, intrinsic, totally untouchable source of inner power—a source that will teach you how to become a centered source of your own self-growth, a practitioner of burgeoning awareness through the life you lead amongst those around you, and experience an ongoing spiritual expansion into love, beauty and truth—you must write. Now, I don't throw around "musts" and "shoulds" very often. And, as a writer, I'm also biased.

You see, throughout the extent of my life, writing has always been a friend. Writing was a friend before I knew it was a friend. I grew up like most kids (at least, that's what I tell myself): I was often confused, hurt, betrayed and a victim—from youthful heartbreak to repressive high school teachers, friendships gone awry and infuriating sports coaches, I long thought that I was a victim of circumstance and others and things far beyond my own control. During the toughest times, the emotions and thoughts would pour out of me uncontrollably—and I needed a place to mop up the mess. I found that space on a blank page.

I would not write often, perhaps once or twice every few months. But in these earliest days of embracing the art of writing as a tool of order, peace and understanding, my young self began to mature and slowly realized that I wasn't ever a victim. I was just playing one.

I played a victim as a kid because I didn't know any better. I never realized that I had the power to choose. Writing began to teach me that power—the power that I always had within me.

These years later, I have come to believe that writing is the most divine of all art forms. Beyond all other mediums and forms of human communication, writing is an extraordinary means of becoming deeply attuned to one's own truth, beliefs, ideals, and aspirations—far beyond sharing simple messages and telling stories. The act of writing is itself an act of understanding. By putting pen to paper, you're engaging in a very reflective and sometimes even confrontational practice of facing your own truth: everything etched within your soul. This is a scary proposition for us. For some reason, we'd rather not know what lies beneath the surface and wonder than to start digging and discover a truth that we can't unsee.

The good news is that writing will unearth every ounce of your spirit, your joy, and your love—just as much as it will help you unearth every ounce of fear, worry, and insecurity that we are each bound by in this human experience. As you write and explore the depths of yourself, you will encounter every dread and anxiety that has ever plagued your subconscious; you will touch every shred of hope that has ever made your heart beat. You will touch every bit of pain that has ever scraped your skin and each taste again each taste of love that has ever graced your lips. And in that explorative process, writing is teaching you that you have the choice to choose what to say, what to share, and what to believe.

As you dig, will learn. And once unearthed, you can choose what to keep around, and what to let go.

Writing is a "sieve" as my friend Rona says, one through which ten million thoughts and ideas and emotions pass every day. What's left when these seemingly chaotic and endless intangibles pass through the sieve is the finest, purest of them all.

Writing cultivates order. Peace. Understanding.

From the upturned soil, new life is breathed into components of your soul that you likely never knew existed. The more you write, the deeper you go. The more you interpret, the more you comprehend. The harder you question, the closer the answers become. Writing provides this personal, powerful catalyst of introspective growth and awareness. And your power begins there: within.

Friend, I know that writing is a tough gig. The process is as erratic and unpredictable as the weather. But its effect upon you is always good. Writing gives you the means to understand how a human being living in this unpredictable, curious existence retains the choice and ability to cultivate simple order and understanding from the natural chaos of thought, circumstances, and life itself. You empower yourself to reinterpret the world, its events, and your life within it—one of six billion upon a swirling marble in an endless night. And that power is truly priceless.

Writing binds the endless landscape of creativity and dreaming and imagination into some rudimentary semblance of cohesion—and if only for a moment, if only for one passing soul to taste it before moving onward in her life, that cohesion is enough to help you give thanks for the remarkable fact that you are here, alive, a part of this existence for just long enough to taste what you desire, to share it with the world, and to do your loving part in support of what is good, just, and true.

No matter the extent of your relationship with writing, I am confident that writing can be that ever-present friend who will teach you how to love yourself. Of course, when you step back and realize that the friend is you, you discover an important truth that we often take for granted: that we are always the ones in power in our own lives.

Dave Ursillo Jr. is a multi-published author and entrepreneur who helps creative self-starters live their leadership every day through writing, business, and artistry. He is the founder of The Literati Writers℠, a premium-membership, online writing community for writers of all levels who want to "live and love" their creative journeys, every step of the way. Find Dave on Twitter @DaveUrsillo and join his mission to discover how to make your creative journey its own reward at LiteratiWriters.com.

THE EMERGING WRITER: Concluding Thoughts

By Dave Ursillo

Standing up and standing out is not enough.

That's what the young, inexperienced writer has not yet learned. The Emerging Writer is engaged in a personal battle with self-belief. The more she stands up for herself and stands out to say, "This is me," the further she goes in committing to herself — perhaps for the very first time. The Emerging Writer thus emerges from her shell: the dark enclave that is protecting but suffocating, an insulating cavern that is keeping her safe from risk and hurt, but which is also isolating her from the experience, depth, nuance, and artistry she craves to feel throughout her life — in writing and beyond. Artistry is not only a calling, but is also a way to feel the love, purpose, and fulfillment that beckon her heart.

So she emerges. And the wall named Fear is faced down — because the writer has faced herself. You could say, "She has found the sun." And although the Emerging Writer now stands gloriously in the sunlight with her arms raised and chest puffed proudly to the sky... nothing happens.

She waits. Still nothing happens.

But she has emerged, hasn't she? She has stood in the face of her fears and worries and all of her doubts and insecurities, has she not? She didn't listen to those who said that art was not a lifestyle, that writing is dead, and that no one reads books anymore. What she is waiting for is for her emergence to reward her: she may not know it but, all along, she quietly expected that emerging from her enclave and standing up for herself for the first time would be the only tough battle. She was wrong.

Although her fears have been faced down, a slow trickle of doubt begins to creep back in — because she looks around and sees that she has not won any merit or accolade from the world around her. The only battle she has won has been with herself, and herself alone.

The Emerging Writer's first battle was indeed with belief — but the battle was only waged within herself. Sure, family and friends might praise her for following her dreams or warn her of the inherent in choosing this writer's life. Perhaps the Emerging Writer now has readers of her own writing, fans even. But the Emerging Writer's great battle with belief is a battle won or lost by her own self-belief, and not the beliefs of others.

Self-belief is the most paramount asset any writer can acquire. But an artist can only acquire this self-belief through the slow, measured process of creating and sharing her art with the world, so that the artist herself is seen. Self-belief cannot be bought or happened upon; it cannot be forged in a few words or proven to others before it is proven to the self. Emerging means standing up and standing out, time after time, and being seen by the world around her. But just because she is standing and is being seen by others does not mean that they care or believe in her, or find her to be the source of their own change, growth, or faith.

Although attaining self-belief is paramount, we often forget that championing this personal battle means so little to those souls around us who are, just as we, striving and fighting to survive. They are dreaming and battling their own fears. They are pursuing better lives and wishing for peace and happiness. The Emerging Writer must remember that achieving one's own self-belief does not make evangelists of onlookers who are, as you were, desperate to simply believe in themselves.

Emerging is about teaching yourself to believe in you, to believe that you are worthy of your earnest desires and dreams. It's about learning that you do indeed have messages within your soul that are worth sharing with the world. It's about finding the humility to understand that others will gladly receive them, when both you and they are ready.

It's writing that helps you accomplish the feat of self-belief. For writing is a practice in self-commitment. The art is a religion in choosing yourself. Each and every time you put pen to paper, you are committing a brazen act of self-belief. And day after day, the practice reaffirms that you have the willpower and the ability to harness the power of writing to make order of disorder; to create peace and understanding from chaos; to forge beauty and truth and love when it is all the easier to avoid the words, or to resist your calling, or to acquiesce to the creative struggle, or to give up and cast stones from frustration.

And once the Emerging Writer discovers this place of self-belief that is forged from writing, she will soon find herself at the precipice of the first evolution of her writer's journey: committing, and committing to more than just herself.

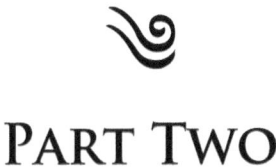

PART TWO

The Committing Writer

THE COMMITTING WRITER

By Dave Ursillo

Back in that dark and damp enclave, our young writer knew that riches and promise lay somewhere beyond that pupil-searing wall of light. She was still terrified of it. She knew that others could pass through it. Day after day, others like her would return to the cave with a bounty of foods and fruits. But she did not know if she was capable of conquering it herself.

Still, they who conquered their own fears returned every evening with riches not found in that cave. And so, she reasoned: "If I emerge, I too will find that bounty and be able to share those riches with others."

She emerges.

And so the Emerging Writer now steps out from her dark cave and into the sunlight. As her eyes adjust to the brightness, she sees something unexpected lie before her: not chests of gold or piles of food ripe for the picking, but an empty field of dirt.

The Emerging Writer sees that field of dirt and feels dismay. She was promised rewards for facing down her fears and emerging from the darkness—or so she thought. The Committing Writer, however, looks upon that expansive space of soil and sees endless promise. This is the ripe ground where anything and everything can be grown: through hard work, patience, perseverance, navigating the terrain, and managing the elemental circumstances that nature will provide.

WHO IS THE COMMITTING WRITER?

The Committing Writer is writing with something to prove. Beyond her own self-belief, she continues to write to make believers out of others around her. She is a worker, a hustler, a provider, and a cultivator. She turns dirt into gold. She sees an empty page and makes it sing. She is professional in demeanor and in practice—which means she is not just writing for herself, but writing for others, too. She has evolved from an unsure and uncertain writer whose words were acts of self-belief forged from self-expression, occasionally looked upon by passersby. She has evolved into a confident and sure-footed creative who is believed in more and more with every passing day. Why? Because she's doing the work. Her writing is doing her talking.

But who, exactly, is the Committing Writer? She already calls herself a writer. She already knows she's a writer. But she is also beginning to understand that achieving her goals of artistry and creative freedom—feeling the depths of purpose and fulfillment that can only be achieved by feeling liberated to say whatever she must say—will require her to accept a few hard truths. Hard truths like the fact that she will not be rewarded just for showing up. That raw self-belief doesn't garnish a payday.

The Committing Writer understands that to continue her creative journey beyond simple self-expression and ordinary self-belief, she needs to branch out from her own humble shell and use her writing to enter the lives of others. She must write for others. Perhaps her writing takes the form of blogging and eBooks. Perhaps her writing takes the form of copy for a variety of customers and clients. Perhaps she buckles down to write her first 60,000-word book. The Committing Writer is deepening her professionalism, and professionalism necessarily involves others, because it requires the opinions, interactions, feedback, and even dollars of others to be made real.

Whatever her expression of professionalism becomes, the Committing Writer understands that it is time to go much, much bigger: beyond a strict, personal, "me"-oriented practice, the Committing Writer is entering a space where she values the opinions and beliefs of others. But committing is a difficult practice that requires tough skin. She is required to regiment her writing practices and impose upon herself some creative constraints—because total freedom can be paralyzing, and healthy routines and habits help her produce and improve. The Committing Writer can no longer afford to treat her craft like a hobby; she must commit more seriously to writing across the board in her life.

The Emerging Writer thought that being seen by others for her self-belief and determination would be enough to prove something to the world. She assumed that, because so few around are willing to stand up as she did (and subject herself to batterings of self-doubt, fear, and criticism from others as she did), she would soon reap the rewards her writer's heart desired. She assumed wrong.

The Committing Writer understands now that you win nothing by standing and being seen—that self-belief is just fundamental. It's the earliest, simplest, and most basic beginning point. And although so few are willing to step into themselves in spite of all the fears and doubts that haunt their weary minds, emerging into the sunlight is not a feat in itself worthy of the praises, songs, or admirations of others.

Emerging doesn't make your words any more worth reading, or sharing, or remembering. It's the practice of commitment that begins to make your words worth reading. It's the practice of commitment that makes your words worth sharing. It's the practice of commitment that makes you, your message, and your ideas worthy of being remembered in a busy, noisy, cluttered, and competitive world.

Commitment is professionalism in practice. And professionalism requires an elevation in creative performance (from writing more, sharing words with more and more eyes, using criticisms to improve your craft, harnessing praise to understand what people value in your style, voice, and approach, etc.) and an elevation in personal standards for the work you create (pursuing higher levels of achievement, garnishing more consistent satisfaction from readers, clients, and customers, etc.).

Committing is a troubling mountain for writers, especially when they have just emerged from their enclaves of doubt and fear. Committing requires significant promises to oneself, and promises to others. But to become a source of love, light, and bravery as a writer, you must go well beyond emerging, and commit. Committing will deepen your practice and guide you to harness a fuller extent of the power of writing. Committing will guide you to become the conduit of love that you are capable of becoming who, now, through your words and in the life you lead, can sow goodness and strength wherever you lay your ink.

I'm a Writer, Damn It!

By Milo McLaughlin

The path to becoming a writer is rarely linear, especially if we lack confidence. We can spend years doubting our writing abilities as we oscillate wildly between the deep inner conviction that we were born for greatness and the sneaking suspicion that we're completely deluding ourselves.

In my life so far, there's been ample evidence for both arguments.

At school, I had an extremely supportive teacher named Mrs. Bliss who deemed my writing ability "close to genius" on a report card. I didn't know this at the time, however, because my parents—perhaps not wanting my head to swell to an unbearable size, or not wanting to set me up for disappointment later in life—hid the report card from me.

When I eventually found out, I thought to myself, sadly, "if only I had known at the time." In the ensuing years, self-doubt had become my constant companion, and creative writing had gone from a joyous, unselfconscious act of expression to a repressed memory.

Epic Storylines

I didn't grow up with a clear idea of what I wanted to do with my life. I had no ambition to be a doctor, lawyer, or famous soccer player. I just wanted to read and play with my Star Wars action figures in the bath, where I would invent epic storylines centered on the bounty hunter Boba Fett (who was clearly the best character, thanks to his mysterious mask and jetpack). I'd like to think this was evidence of a natural flair for storytelling. I also made my own comics and sold them to our neighbors, who mainly bought them because I incorporated their pet cats as recurring characters.

This creative tendency also surfaced when I was at school. I wrote stories about tightrope walkers who had fatal accidents, and about the sadness of family secrets locked in attics and relationships gone sour, the kind of stuff a 9-year-old kid probably shouldn't be thinking or writing about.

Mrs. Bliss had me read my stories out loud in front of the class and even let me skip sports class so I could write more. It may not have added to my street cred, but it was great to have someone believe in me. Without that early encouragement, I might never have gone back to writing later on.

Slapped Down Mercilessly

Then we moved from urban England to rural Ireland and, at 11 years old, I started life at a different school, a school where large wooden rulers were slapped down mercilessly on heads and hands if you were judged not to be paying attention.

A self-conscious teenager and a fish out of water, I suddenly became aware that showing enthusiasm about schoolwork was not a good way to fit in. Looking back, it's clear to me that I began to "hide my light under a bushel" when it came to creativity and writing. I affected a studied air of indifference that soon became second nature.

I somehow ended up spending my lunchtimes sitting with the boring kids who talked about their Sega Megadrives while I quietly chewed my tuna sandwiches. My dad told me we couldn't afford a games console, but I still half-expected to see one on Christmas morning and was inconsolable (no pun intended) when it didn't appear. I couldn't care less about playing games; I just wanted to fit in.

Hazy Memories

We moved back to a nearby city when I was about 14 and I made new friends through an acting class I attended. I also became acquainted with Nirvana and the Red Hot Chili Peppers, Reservoir Dogs and Rage Against the Machine. And beer. My parents also separated around this time, causing a whirlwind of confusing emotions I tried to block out. My attitude became increasingly nihilistic and hedonistic.

I came up with a good ruse for getting drunk, despite still being a skinny 15-year-old. I would call the cab/taxi company and affect a deeper voice. I would ask for them to go and buy a 12-pack of lager and deliver it to my house. To my surprise, they agreed!

When the cab/taxi driver arrived, I would open the door and they'd ask for my dad. I'd say he was in the shower, but that he had given me the money for the beer. Seeing as the driver had already gone to the trouble of buying it, he didn't ask too many questions. I suddenly became more popular.

We would sit around in my pal's back garden drinking those horrible, warm beers out of the can and smoking cigarettes. It was a laugh and I began to come out of my shell a bit. At school, I also gravitated toward a more hedonistic crew. On a fairly typical lunchtime, we drank cheap cider down by the river and drunkenly kicked a football around, resulting in my puking the cider right back up. I haven't been able to drink the stuff since.

On the last day of school, after a mediocre performance on our exams, we got caught by the principal drinking round the back, and he chased us off the school grounds, him driving after us, the front bumper of his car at our heels as we ran, laughing so much we could barely breathe.

During this era of drunken shenanigans, writing seemed like something I did in a past life.

Adrift in the World

Just before I turned 17, I left Ireland to study in Scotland, where I continued to drink stupid amounts of alcohol and behave terribly. Three years into my four-year degree, I realized how bad things had become and decided to make a change. I discovered a book called The Artist's Way and tried meditation. The combination of the two helped me cut back on drinking and begin writing again—mainly Dylanesque lyrics and a few short stories, plus some articles for the college magazine.

One year later, my girlfriend and I graduated and found ourselves adrift in the world with little clue what to do next. We both took on whatever work we could find, which for me was a string of dead-end jobs including working in a record store, at a call center, and as an administrator for the Scottish civil service.

In addition to these various day jobs, I dabbled in music and started writing for several local magazines. I met someone with a blog and was inspired to start my own.

The years went by and I remained a civil servant. The problem was that most of the writing I was doing was either for free or for very little money, and I felt no closer to being able to leave my job to be a writer.

Eventually, however, I decided not to work for free anymore, and to focus on making my blog more professional. Because of this, I began to get offered some extra work, both as a production journalist for a newspaper and as a copywriter for a creative agency. After nine years as a civil servant, I cut down my hours to four days a week and worked in the agency on Mondays.

The Big Decision

Working elsewhere one day a week gave me an insight into a whole new world where I could be creative and earn decent money. This was fantastic, but made the other four days of the week at my old job unbearable.

I'd been promoted several times over the years, going from a poorly paid administrative assistant to a digital communications role with a decent paycheck.

But most of my day was spent filtering enormous amounts of email and struggling to push forward my ideas. I felt that positive progress was made impossible by a mind-boggling array of bureaucratic procedures and internal politics. It got to the point where I would stare out of the window at the huge container ships coming and going from the docks and wish I could also be transported somewhere else.

As I thought back to how I'd ended up in this situation, I realized I'd consistently given up on what I really cared about for job security and a comfortable lifestyle. Those decisions had seemed sensible at the time but had only made me miserable in the long-term. When management announced they were letting people go and paying a severance package, I decided to take the plunge.

On February 3, 2012, 10 years after I first became a civil servant, I walked out of that big soulless government building a free man. I had committed to a new life of writing for a living.

The real hard work was about to begin.

Since leaving, I've quit drinking, taken up meditation again, run a half-marathon, and self-published six eBooks. I've had some teething problems with my freelance writing business as I experiment with different ways of working, but the important thing is that I can now proudly say, "I'm a writer, damn it!"

I strongly suspect that if you're reading this, you are, too—I just hope you don't wait as long as I did to start believing it.

Milo McLaughlin *is a former civil servant forging a new path in life as a content creator. He strongly believes that writers and other creative people can make a good living from work that is enjoyable and meaningful to them, but that it takes patience, determination, and a willingness to change limiting habits and beliefs. In 2011, Milo founded ClearMindedCreative.com to share his own journey and provide inspiration, support, and practical advice to other creative types in search of a more fulfilling life and career.*

Don't Stop Writing Now

By Cassia Cogger

do not consider myself a writer, but I find it essential to write. To clear my mind. To make some space. To put thoughts and dreams into something concrete on a page. To find my way. As a painter, when I can't quite figure out how to say something visually, to communicate in brush strokes, I sit down. I put my pen to page or my fingers to my keyboard or even my thumbs to my iPhone. I start to write and the answers reveal themselves. The how-tos. The must-dos. Then, I go back to my piece and know just how to finish it.

As a human, I don't always learn everything I need to do while in the midst of an experience. It is after, when I sit with it, when I write about it, that many lessons are revealed. For me, writing is about expression. Through expression, I find connection to myself, to others, and to the actual environment around me.

It hasn't always been this way. For over 15 years, I participated in programs and courses. I traveled and threw myself into a number of experiences. Journaling was always a recommended part. I never did it. I felt that I could process things in my head. I always said I was too busy. Now, however, I realize there was safety in not writing things down. If I didn't record something, maybe it wasn't real.

But when you refuse to confirm the reality of an experience, you can't really let it go. How do you say goodbye to something that (allegedly) isn't real?

Somehow, spilling the words, experiences, and thoughts out onto the page gives them form. It then makes room for more thoughts, new thoughts. My ideas are able to grow and shift once put down on the page. They are able to turn upside down and all around once I release them from me and can witness them on a page. I don't always, or even often, know where they will end up, and sometimes that can be scary.

Like all good things, however, this fear is what makes it exciting. It's scary because it matters. It's scary because it is a connection with the self and, once you tune in to your heart's song, once you begin to document it, it demands more and more attention until you align with it. In this alignment, you find peace.

In this alignment, you find magic.

So maybe you're a writer. Maybe you're not. Either way, don't quit writing now. It is so much more than the action of putting words to the page. It is a practice to process ideas and dreams. An opportunity to begin to know yourself. A way to share your stories with others and create connection. As you connect with others, you can come full circle and connect more fully with yourself.

Cassia Cogger is a mother and wife by sweet and sacred luck, an Internet expert by default, a former ironman by sweat and determination, a poet on purpose, and an artist by soul. She looks to catch stars wherever she goes. All of the above are totally related, and someday she might even tell us how. Until then, she's still figuring it all out. One of her tools for this self-exploration is writing.

Unleash Your Word Dragon

By Lisa Landtroop

You know you have one. As writers, we all have a hidden dragon lurking within our soul. It's time once again to let it breathe fire into your pages. Unleash your inner dragon by sharing your glorious story-telling talents with the world! If that doesn't sound like the kind of writing you're capable of, just indulge me for a moment.

It is often said that a picture is worth a thousand words. So why, then, do people always say that the book was so much better than the movie? Because words give us the power to visualize a story in our mind's eye. And the mind's eye has much more depth and breadth than our actual eyes.

You're a writer because the stories you like to write are enchanting. They're engaging. Sometimes, they're even enlightening. You love to entertain and/or educate. You bask in the thrill of eliciting an emotional connection with others. You know that the stories of life are best told by those who possess the powerful gift of words. You fiercely believe with all of your being that words set one's soul ablaze with a fiery passion – that same fiery passion that dragons use to spew forth their flames.

So why do you feel like quitting? You've worked so hard to cultivate your voice, but now you may be feeling lost, tired, or even burnt out. It's completely normal to hit a spot in the road where you question your abilities, your motives, and even your drive to continue. It happens to every writer, often more than once.

Why, then, do you continue writing?

Because your desire to write continues to burn, no matter how tired you feel. You know there are others out there who are making their writing dreams come true, so why can't you? You can. You can make it. If you don't give up.

So how can you unleash your very own inner word dragon?

First, review your own favorite piece of written work. Relive how you felt as you wrote the words. Where were you? What was going on in your life at that moment? What emotions were prevalent? Let the words transport you back to that place in your life. Savor the memory. Feel the flames lapping against your face once again.

Next, read your favorite story from a different author. Think about why you love the story. Is it the complex character development? Is it the description of the world that exists around the characters? Is it the fantasy, or the fact that it dances around reality just enough to fully transport you into the story? Is it the dragons? Enjoy the words again. Feel, really feel, how they make you experience wonderfully rich emotions.

Then? The answer is so simple, it's almost maddening. No one ever told you it would be easy, but it truly is quite simple.

Keep writing.

When we dare to express ourselves, to expose our weakest vulnerabilities, there are times when we feel raw—and quite possibly even battered or bruised—by sharing our words, much like a dragon shedding its scaly skin, or struggling through a zealous battle, aflame with the blistering heat of its opponent.

When our writing appears to fall on deaf ears, it leaves us feeling more alone than anything else. For you see, we are writers, you and I. And writing fulfills us to the core of our being. We write because we long to share. And when that sharing doesn't produce the results we had hoped for... we ache. But through the pain, we grow.

Yes, we grow.

Please don't quit writing. You have an indisputable love for words. Otherwise, you wouldn't feel so alone and desperate right now. You wouldn't be wondering whether or not you should quit if you didn't love what you do so passionately, igniting a burning desire in others to also share their most vulnerable and searing moments.

Your beautiful words are meaningful to all of those who lack the gift of expressing themselves through words. It may be hard to comprehend that others cannot just hammer out a story, a poem, a love letter, a sonnet, a rant, or a song as eloquently and effortlessly as you. But the vast majority of the world is woefully lacking in the art of storytelling.

Yet they love reading stories.

You have a remarkable gift. Whoever imparted in you the love of words did the world a great and invaluable service. Please don't withhold your talents from those who know not how to express themselves poetically.

Just write. Find a reason, a will, a way, and just write. Like a dragon flying onward, keep writing and your vision will soon burn bright within your soul once again.

Lisa Landtroop owns BXLNT (Be eXceLleNT), a multi-platform enterprise specializing in time awareness coaching, copywriting, editing, and proofing to encourage and support change leaders. She is the creator of the powerful course Take Your Life Back, which helps change-makers remember that life is too short to do stuff you hate. Connect with Lisa on Twitter @LisaLandtroop and reach her by email at lisa@tqltotalqualitylife.com.

FEAR AND THE WRITER'S JOURNEY

By Jessica Glendinning

The conversation usually goes something like this:

"So, you call yourself a 'writer,' huh?"
    "Yes. Yes, I do!"
"What gives you the right? Who do you think you are?"
    "Um."
"What makes you any different from all the others who have tried and failed before you?"
    "Well. I…"
"Why bother even trying? You know you're going to fail, right? Far better writers than you have fallen flat on their faces, writers who have more talent in their little finger than you have in that entire brain of yours. The odds are stacked against you."
    "… *whimper*"
"Yeah. Good luck with that. Maybe you should quit while you're ahead, step back in line, and go get a real job. It's not like you're going to make it anyway."

It may be a bit of an exaggeration, and the conversation is probably different every time it happens, but my guess is that a lot of us have the same conversation repeatedly inside our own heads, with many different variations and with differing degrees of self-deprecation. The main characters in this continuing saga are you, the writer, and your old friend FEAR.

FEAR is a bastard. He likes to come around, uninvited and at inopportune moments. He likes to crash the party just when things are getting fun, just when you are starting to let go and enjoy yourself, right around the time you have dipped your toes in the water and have made the decision to jump in. It's around this point that he struts in, takes one look into your eyes, and it's all over. He has this way of wrapping his cold, sinewy hand around your heart that takes your breath away, sends a chill down into your guts, and causes you to freeze up. He takes the joy you get from writing and ruthlessly smashes it to bits, making you second-guess your abilities. You watch helplessly as your confidence withers away. By the time he has his way with you, if you let him, you are left a whimpering mess, your words a mere memory and your motivation long gone. Seriously—who were you to think you could make it as a professional writer?

Chances are, FEAR has brought you close to quitting more times than you can count. But before you quit writing, let's take a moment to reflect and reset. It's time to change the conversation. It's time to take our good friend FEAR and welcome him inside. But this time, instead of letting him waltz in and ruin everything, channel the negative energy he brings with him and turn it into fuel for the long road ahead. Standing on the edge of that cliff can be terrifying. Making the commitment to take your writing seriously can feel like jumping over a vast, dark chasm with no safety net. But it can also be one of the most exhilarating experiences of your life.

Our friend FEAR may be just the signpost we've been looking for along our journey; he may be telling us that what we are doing is exactly what we are supposed to be doing. That tremor of uncertainty? Chances are, the sense of trepidation is a precursor to the sensation of freedom and possibility that wait just around the corner when we take the leap into the next stages of our writing.

Instead of letting FEAR dominate us, we can use him for guidance and then leave him behind. We can move forward without him, knowing he has shown us the way.

It's time to move forward, without that questioning voice inside our heads, that twist in our guts. It's time for you to make the transition from "writer" to WRITER. It's time for the ink to flow, for the words to carry you along on your journey, to start your evolution. It's time, dear writer, for you to live your story.

I can't wait to read it.

Jessica Glendinning is a seeker. A designer, writer, yogi, activist, and musician, passionate and a perfectionist, she adores alliteration and all things fuzzy. She grew up a weird kid, then lost herself somewhere along the way. Several years ago, she woke up, detached from society's expectations, and embraced her non-conformity. Her life is a constant evolution, a journey of discovery and improvement. She hopes to find herself somewhere along the way. Her one constant is this: she knows she is here to save the world. She can be found online at VerdantSpringDesign.com.

Write What You Wish to Read

By Lauryn Doll

I've always loved books. Always. So much so that I taught myself how to read.

I slept with books in my bed, carried them with me wherever I went, and even read them in class instead of paying attention to my schoolwork. Even now, when at the mall, I spend most of my time in the bookstore instead of the clothing stores.

Despite all of this, writing wasn't an immediate passion of mine. Yes, I love to express myself, but I'm not a grammar Nazi. I'm not caught up on sentence structure and styling. And while spelling's important, sometimes you can forgive a little *slanguage* when artfully applied. Plus, I never fashioned myself as artistic, or felt myself desirous of the writer's life.

You know why I started writing?

Because I wanted money, damn it.

Blogs, articles, Kindle books. I wrote them all for money. Yeah, I vented on CrushSpot or MySpace but, when it came to really writing, making money online was my focus. I wanted money here and now, and I didn't want to make it in a cubicle. As long as writing kept money in my pocket and kept my schedule flexible, I was all for it.

I got a real taste of freedom and flexibility when I produced a Kindle book on sex in one afternoon. I loved sex books. I loved to talk about sex. I thought—and still think—it's something we all need to function and thrive. So I wrote about it.

I threw that little book out there and grossed thousands of dollars in sales over the next year and a half. I lived on that money. I didn't worry about my bills because of that money. I chilled out and lived well (in my head) off that money.

But then things shifted.

I took a hit in sales, which extended into a steady decline. After several months, I finally looked into why my sales had dropped. Part of it was insufferable laziness. I didn't reinvest earnings into marketing and improvement. The other part was that I had failed to write the book I wanted to read.

When you write for financial gain, you tend not to think about your audience. Or at least not enough. You think only about yourself, and about how much money you need to make in order to continue doing everything you want to do.

The best books, however—the ones that are classics, timeless in appeal—are the books that weren't written for money, but out of passion and desire. To inform. To educate. To entertain. To seduce. To transform. To express.

Hemingway didn't become an American prolific because he put a picture of the new house and Porsche he wanted on his desk and speed-wrote his way to glory. He examined his life, and that of others, and married the simple with the profound, the clean with the profane. He took the time to craft from his soul.

Sex is an important topic in our society. It is one I consider oversaturated with fluff, yet underserved with realness and authenticity. I believe my initial books, while short and rushed, were successful *because* I was real and authentic. After reading, people emailed me, sharing their thoughts on my work, and asking more questions. They found my voice open, sexy, and refreshing. Still, I realized that, in rushing the book, I had not given them enough.

I've spent quite some time during my writing hiatus exploring the art of creation, of writing, and of connecting. I read

The Artist's Way and Kleon's *How to Steal Like an Artist*. In reading the latter, I had an *aha* moment.

Kleon's tip to "write the book you want to read" made things clear for me. Writing what you like to write about is more important than writing what you know about. When you write what you want to read, you to see where your heart is and where your passion lies. When you write like this *and* consider the audience you're serving, you give them everything they could ever dream to ask for—and more.

When I looked at my already-published books, I realized they were good, but they weren't what I wanted to read. I provided a basic foundation, but there were things I wanted to add. Real stories. Advice from actual people. Applicable techniques that hadn't already been thrown into every beginner's manual. A luxurious, sensual, funny, entertaining, brain-and-toe-tingling experience from cover to cover.

I wanted something that was insatiable in its giving. And what I produced was anything but. What I currently had was the equivalent of 60 seconds of amazing sex from a selfish lover who didn't come back for a round two but, instead, turned on SportsCenter and acted as if nothing was wrong.

Ouch.

Think about what it means to create the ultimate book on your topic or genre. Look at the timeless classics. If you're not sure what to write, imagine the last book you read that failed to meet your expectations, preferably in your genre. Why did it suck? What would have made it better? How can you excel with your book so that readers won't feel this way about you?

For me, titles like *The Sensuous Woman by J* or *The Joy of Sex* are my case studies. If I were to make something of this caliber, how would I do so?

Well, I guess you'll just have to wait and see when I publish it.

Lauryn Doll *is the sexy Digital Strategist behind* Wild Topaz Media, *which houses the Lauryn Doll, Sexy Focused Ambitious and Beauty Sex Fitness brands. Lauryn began writing when she was in her late teens to vent frustrations after a very bad breakup and while going through general teen angst. Over time, her colorful way of saying things, coupled with her ability to ask the right questions, earned her a role as Associate Editor of J'ADORE Magazine.*

Let Your Writing Do Your Talking

By Sang Thi Duong

Some may describe me as a cold-hearted bitch. Others may say I am the nicest, sweetest person they have ever met. I say I am adaptable and, whether you rock some Target heels or some Louboutins, if you sashay one step at a time you can project a lot of fierceness. This did not come easy to me. It has been a daunting journey. From the girl who once owned every Nike Air Max to the lady who now owns more than 300 pair of heels, I take my feelings out on words. I let the words do the talking and I write with the wind—just like I strut.

You see, when I was younger, I was abused, verbally, mentally, and physically. My dad told me how much he could not stand me. He lashed out at me. He tainted my mind with low self-worth. In my house, we were not allowed to speak of feelings, thoughts, or even opinions. Each night, I wanted to escape the hell I was living in and live in the land of magic and unicorns.

I escaped every night to this fantasy by writing.

I wrote my feelings. I wrote my thoughts. I wrote my opinions. I wrote my dreams and wishes for the future. I wrote to release my anger. I wrote to be happy. I wrote to be who I truly was on paper. I wrote to be free.

After leaving home, I wrote more and more, because I landed myself in one abusive relationship after another. I wrote until I was betrayed. Some evil being took my words and strewed them across walls, ripping out the pages of my heart. A piece of me died that day. I stopped writing. I refused to write. It took me nearly 10 years before I felt able to write my words again. This time, I wrote to share my life and my experiences, and to help others heal. Now I write on my own terms. And I take my writings to the streets. Literally. By writing, I snatched my words off the paper and became BOLD and FIERCE, live and in person.

I am not going to lie. At first, I was scared shitless to speak my mind, because I feared someone would strike me down. I broke this barrier and learned to LOVE myself and embrace who I was on the inside. The little girl who was trapped in those journals was released into the wild world of openness.

I challenge you to write what makes you happy, what makes you sad, what makes you think, and what pisses you off. I challenge you to write whatever the hell you want.

Here are a few writing missions (should you choose to accept them):

- Send your lover an old-fashioned, handwritten love note. Take the words that bind your heart and put them on paper. Allow your thoughts to roam free.

- Get a Kick-Ass Journal. Go out and buy a journal, or even a plain old notebook. In this journal, write down shit you really want to say. If you ever find yourself censoring yourself, stop. Then write what you REALLY wanted to say. BE HONEST!

- Write your life story. Write about all the good, bad, ugly, and absolutely amazing times of your life. These experiences made you who you are today. Write pieces as they come to you. Trust me. You'll love it. Plus, your kids or your kids'

kids will love to read a little bit of family history.

Each day that passes, despite the ways in which the past presents its ugly face to me, writing helps me realize that I am exactly where I am supposed to be. Boldy. Fiercely. Proudly. And I love that.

Sang Thi Duong is a speaker, rock star scribe, and event social media commander. She is the founder of Sangtastik, where she canvasses the pavement in her Ferrari Red Heels and flowing satin scarf. Sang also teaches youth entrepreneurship and mentors teenage girls. When Sang is not networking, writing, or reading, she can be found taking time to breathe and living life while sipping on some Starbucks.

I Write to Liberate

By Kadena Tate

My truth stands in front of me, begging to be heard. It pleads with me to pour my soul out onto a blank piece of paper. My pen purrs softly, beckoning to every piece of me and whispering in my ear, "Relax your breath. Let me explore your mind. Let me arouse and claim your inner weakness of honesty."

I wince, my heart races, and a feeling of anxiety courses through my body as I stare at the words. The room is spinning so fast. I can hear the sound of my blood running through my body. Yet the words flow so freely: "Words are the currency of the web." I ponder the sweet possibility of one day, very soon, being able to communicate with clarity, brevity, love, and authority.

This is a delicious thought because I know deep within that words can uplift, inspire, encourage, empower, and equip myself and others with the inspiration and motivation necessary to create an amazing life. This thought strengthens me. I straighten my back as the fear attempts to slither up my spine and flood my brain with the belief that my words are ineffective, inadequate, and irrelevant.

I take slow, deep breaths and remember that being "unapologetically me" releases me from the bondage of self-hatred. I look into the mirror and remember that it is words that undress me. My pen performs a slow striptease, allowing each word to rise to the surface, naked and unashamed, allowing me to free my thoughts.

Thoughts bubble up endlessly from a reservoir deep within, longing to be fully embraced. Many emotions rise to the surface: hurt, anger, happiness, sadness, confusion, delusion, fear, romance, greed, calm.

But they all appear as frightened words trying to escape the pen, unwilling to fall onto the paper, fearing that judgment may ensue.

I calm down and tell my soul that every word is a treasure. I must write because there are millions and millions of words hidden in my head, and within the crevices of my heart, yearning to be heard, to be seen, to encourage and to empower.

So I take my power back and I write. I write about what makes me laugh, cry, and cringe. I write about what brings me freedom, and what keeps me in bondage. I write until every fiber in my being no longer resists creativity but, rather, screams, cries, and begs for it. Sentences fly out of my mind.

That's why I write: for others to feel liberated and release the false belief that they cannot do what they dream, that they cannot be themselves, or that they do not have enough. Through vivid writing, you set captive thoughts free—and that is what moves others to action. Words are meant to be read and interpreted to fit one's own life, and you never know whose life you will touch by choosing to share your words.

Kadena Tate is a creative visionary and change agent who uses coaching, consulting, speaking, and training to help entrepreneurs leapfrog the market and make the competition irrelevant. Contributing author in the NYT Bestseller Business Model You, Kadena believes that authenticity has no competition. As a business acceleration alchemist, she will help you gain the confidence and clarity necessary to attract clients, cash, and clout. Visit her online today at KadenaTate.com.

Unexpressed Creativity Bites Back

By Meagan Christine Williams

Writing is a place where I fit. Where I feel at home no matter where I am. Writing isn't something that will walk away. It won't argue with me or hurt my feelings. Writing is my truth expressed. It's a way for me to articulate thoughts when I can't do so vocally. It's where my heart and soul are, where I become inspired and where I create. It's a way to bare my soul to the world and to share the love of people and of life that I have.

Writing doesn't have limits or walls unless I create them. I have complete freedom there. It's a way for me to let go and be out of control if I want. It's there to support me when I succeed and when I fuck up. Writing is a way to release everything I keep stuck deep inside, the parts of me I don't let anyone see. The parts I think people couldn't possibly love me for. Those are the parts that benefit most from my writing.

Something wonderful happens when those dark places are uncovered. Love and connection happen. Creativity and healing begin.

Writing is a place where I can give and give and give and it only fills me up more with love and passion and motivation. It doesn't drain me or take advantage of me. It won't ignore me or hurt me. It only heals. I'm always noticed and appreciated when I spend time with my notebook. It doesn't blow me off or try to change me. It's unconditionally accepting of me and all my emotions. It embraces them and reflects them back in the most beautiful way.

As I made my way through childhood, writing was a gift. As much as I never stood out, I never felt as if I completely fit in either. I was intelligent, but felt as if this didn't always translate vocally.

Writing became my way to communicate.

Growing up, I felt burdened by my intuitiveness and compassion. I constantly took time for others, but didn't get much in return. Eventually, this wore me out and I pulled back. I felt hurt and used by too many people. My heart was broken, but my love for writing helped heal it. It helped me reach out and let people in again.

Writing helped me discover who I am. It helped me bring to the surface everything I didn't want to see at first. Every bit of emotion I had not expressed, every secret, every bit of hurt came out when I was alone with my notebook. My writing slowly broke down the walls I had built tall and strong around my heart. Eventually, I became grateful at seeing my authentic truth revealed.

If I had stopped writing when I thought I wanted to, I would never have discovered how much divinity, beauty, and creativity there is within me, and within every person in the Universe. I want you to discover that too because, once you do, it changes everything.

The way you look at life changes, the way you treat others changes, the way you treat yourself changes, and you realize that despite the challenges that inevitably come along, you are a writer. You are capable of writing great things and touching people's souls. You can heal your heart and lead others to healing as well. All you have to do is let go, open your heart, be vulnerable, and let it flow.

There are plenty of reasons to write, but what it comes down to is knowing YOUR reasons to write. What has it helped you with? How do you feel when you're creating? What do you feel needs to be expressed or uncovered? Writing is a source of creation, inspiration, and connection for me. What will it be for you?

It's important for your soul to be expressed. Unexpressed creativity bites back. So love your creative passions, run toward them, embrace them. It's a wonderful gift. It's well worth any frustrations that may come up. There's a reason you've been drawn to writing. Trust that instinct. Writing doesn't disappoint.

You may walk away from it, but it will follow. It'll pull at your heart and bring you home to your creative soul. You can do this. You have so much within you that is just begging to be shared.

Meagan Christine Williams is a writer, traveler, coach, and lover of people and the Universe. In August 2011, she was on track to become a part of the corporate world but realized something wasn't clicking; she longed for something more. So she quit business school and pursued her desire to change the world by helping people make their dreams come true and better their lives. Today, through writing and coaching, she helps others heal their hearts and discover the beauty and value within themselves, while also exploring her own passions, such as spirituality, creativity, love, and the Universe. She can be found at MeaganCWilliams.com.

THE COMMITTING WRITER: CONCLUDING THOUGHTS

By Dave Ursillo

The Emerging Writer was a subject of fear, quietly cast into bondage by the same perpetual unknown and uncertainty that all human beings must endure. For the writer, this fear is a plague of doubt, worry, unsureness, and insecurity. The Emerging Writer is safe and protected when she ignores the calling to write, whereas embracing her calling is embracing the unknown, uncertainty, her own self-doubt, her own truth, and the words and worries of others around her. Writing is a game played in the hearts and minds of others as much as it is played in the hearts and minds of we who write. The same is said for all artistry: who are artists but those who assign value, emotion, and meaning to the messages, ideas, images, and visages we deem worthy of the eyes and ears of others?

The Emerging Writer must face her fears—and face herself—by walking out from her protected enclave and into the white wall named fear.

But once there, as her pupils adjust to the light and she sees that she has survived a seemingly destitute leap into the unknown, she realizes a startling truth: accepting the nature of this uncertain life, the same circumstance that holds court over every human being, does not make for her own success. She does not win the praise of others for having believed in herself; for having "shown up"; for making only the most basic effort required to stand upon her own feet and say, "I believe in me."

And so committing becomes the task at hand. The Emerging Writer evolves. With self-belief in her holster, however shaky or young that self-belief may feel, she gets to work. The Committing Writer is a practitioner in professionalism and dedicated effort. She has something to prove to the world around her, and proving something to the world takes substantial practice (in the development of her skills and abilities), determination (both strength of mind and the humility to change, innovate, or alter one's path), and consistency over time. She makes statement after statement in her truth-seeking words, in her unrelenting brazenness, and in her caliber of work—a caliber that improves with every stroke of the pen, and by her willingness to accept that her work can always be made better.

But before long, The Committing Writer grows weary. She grows tired. As the weeks turn into months and the months turn into years, her beautiful craft of writing begins to feel like a burden. Her professionalism has led her to success, surely. She has begun to make a living for herself, she has garnished admiration from readers who have discovered her words, and she has earned the genuine respect and support of peers like her.

But the writing itself has begun to suffer. Her ability to be so productive, committed, and professional has turned her artistic craft into a factory line, a high-numbers game of word-count production that serves the needs of others but neglects the ideals, dreams, and values she wanted all along, the motivating beliefs and desires that sparked her to begin this journey in the first place.

The Committing Writer begins to feel she's lost the feeling

of depth, nuance, purpose, artistry, and creative fulfillment she desired long before she emerged from her protected enclave.

Where The Emerging Writer must face herself and battle with her own self-belief, the Committing Writer must face the eyes of others. Earning their respect, however, does not make for a flourishing creative life.

The Committing Writer must evolve. She must go beyond using her writing to appease clients and please readers and satisfy those who view her words and garnish respect from onlookers who pass her by. She must dip into her soul and unearth the very core of what brought her into this journey to begin with. She must infuse her craft with her own creative genius and artistic desires and personal wants and audacious dreams.

She must evolve once again, just as she did from emergence to commitment, to flourish.

PART THREE

The Flourishing Writer

The Flourishing Writer

By Dave Ursillo

If every journey begins by emerging, every journey aspires to reach one destination: flourishing.

Flourishing is a place in the sun. It is a paradise where complementary forces serve both the self and the greater good, a place where a crossroads of personal growth, purposeful work, and life experience fuel creative outputs that positively touch the lives of others. Here, the great white wall named Fear is reduced from its towering, intimidating stature to mere flashes in the night sky, passing bolts that intimidate and cause hesitation and that can surely maim, but which are chosen and pursued. The Flourishing Writer sees each fear as a place where she can most acutely learn, grow, and evolve. Where the storms rage at their most violent, the Flourishing Writer finds a stage upon which few others are willing to stand, perform, and shine. And so she does.

Flourishing is a state of being. While this is the writer's ultimate destination, flourishing is not an outcome or an end goal. It is neither a finish line that can be crossed nor a trophy that can be acquired. Flourishing may well be a paradise, but it is a working paradise, a living practice. Flourishing is a reciprocal state of being where art supports life and life supports art. And every worthy project, essay, and effort ebbs and flows between determined pursuit and simple presence; aggressive growth and total stillness; pursued-risk at the chance of greatness and deep breaths of comfort, gratitude, and simple enjoyment.

To flourish in the creative journey is to experience this ongoing, momentous cycle of progressive self-expansion. The cycle of ebb and flow experienced by the Flourishing Writer allows her to remain aligned to her standards, attuned to her core beliefs, and on task with exactly what she wants and needs—exactly how she wants and needs it.

WHO IS THE FLOURISHING WRITER?

The Flourishing Writer is a veteran of the craft. She may not be an expert of its rules, but she is a teacher of writing all the same. Although she may not be a "professional" in title, she is professional by trade: in demeanor, practice, and experience. Writing is bound up in her personal sense of joy and mission. To write is to feel joy, and that joy is priceless and reaffirming. The self-belief of the Flourishing Writer overrides any fears and doubts that still linger in her (they always will), for she is emboldened by her craft every time she makes the time and space for it. Writing no longer comes at the expense of her mental, emotional, and even financial well-being, but actually contributes to them substantially. And although she is still experiencing various changes and evolutions in her goals, dreams, and desires, writing is now a part of her—and that is not a question. She knows damn well she is a writer in name and, now, she is called to become an artist in stature.

But the Flourishing Writer has her own trials to face.

Looking back, the Emerging Writer began as a young idealist

without a soapbox. What she discovered is that her mission is herself, that her own self-belief is the most fundamental and influential building block upon which her creative journey (and her life's journey) may stand. Trial after trial, doubt after doubt, fear after fear, the Emerging Writer stood up and stood out, but she began to understand that believing in oneself holds little merit in the eyes of others. You win few rewards, points, praises, or cookies for believing in yourself if your worldly work, earthly efforts, and out-of-body contributions to the world around you have paled in comparison. She had to work hard and long to win respect, and to attain practical things, like making money from her craft. And so she committed.

The Committing Writer evolved from youthful worry into a workhorse draped in self-belief. She emerged triumphantly and survived her most pressing doubts, fears, and worries. With continued dedication over the weeks and years, the Committing Writer grew into a champion of her craft: one who was admired by others, respected by peers, and even sought after for professional needs and projects. Every page, every effort, every ounce of ink continued to prove her level of dedication to herself and to her craft. She wrote with passion and professionalism. Motivated by her intrinsic desire to create, she further served her own practical needs by serving the needs of others.

Unlike the Emerging Writer and the Committing Writer, the Flourishing Writer does not face one battle but an ongoing trial: a deepening of practice; an expansion from simple expression into professionalism, and from professionalism into spiritual, soulful experience. The trial is that flourishing is not an outcome. Flourishing is an ongoing process—a cycle of growth and regression. It is a goal and an ideal that are discovered with practice and in practice.

The Flourishing Writer now finds herself at the precipice of evolution. And this new stage of evolution demands a deepening of practice and a fresh recommitment that will align her journey with her earnest desires for artistic freedom and purpose. First, she has little motivation now to turn dissenters into believers, for that is a winless game, a revolving door, a hamster wheel, a shouting match with an undying wind. She has grown tired of creating work with "something to prove"—a shallow, petty, pedantic game of opinion does little to reflect her own motivations, let alone reward her with a sense of purpose or fulfillment.

The Flourishing Writer has also grown to realize that working for the opinions of others is very practical and financially responsible (for few will pay for work they do not like, want, or desire), and yet writing solely to win respect and praise now feels empty and hollow. Her words feel less honest and true than they do simple, safe, sure, and certain. To the Flourishing Writer, the desire to create beauty with meaning and purpose exists far beyond the scale whereupon the outside opinions, emotions, thoughts, and judgments of others lie—a place that is forever and always beyond her own control.

What the Flourishing Writer does want is to return to a time and place when writing was a cherished exercise. Today, and in spite of her successes and leaps forward as a writer, she feels called to escape the entrapments of "production mode" and return her writing to a more spiritual, soulful practice that honors her and nurtures her on a profoundly personal level. She wants to apply all that she has learned and all that she has become to intelligent, creative practices that empower her to live and love a meaningful, deep, and nuanced journey—something she has gotten away from in recent times. By returning to her roots, her voice, and her desires to share a message that influences change in others, she believes in her heart that she will reconnect with what inspired her to begin her creative journey.

Thus, the Flourishing Writer must tap back into her own self-belief to discover the personal standards that guide her sense of purpose, meaning, and fulfillment, the principles and ideals that reflect her values, wants, and desires and that will help her, in practice, honor her creative and artistic desires. Using these soulful measures and metrics to assess and weigh the value, worth, and merit of artistic projects, creative ventures, and even the work she conjures up for clients and customers, she discovers a new depth of cohesion between her art and the mission that has long called to her, that idea, journey, or message that might help, influence, inspire, challenge, or teach the men and women around her who need it, value it, love it, and despise it all the same.

Because what she wishes to create as a writer has shifted, the nature of her work must shift, too. The work that "truly matters" must evolve from pure hustle and production to a concentration of value. She must return to her own voice and allow her truth to surge forth. She must seek creative challenges over what's routine; pursue artistic risks over safety; envelop her journey in mission and purpose over what's expected and merely a popular trend.

The Flourishing Writer evolves when the nature of her art evolves. She must find a mesh between personal desire and the desires of the collective, an infusion of practices that honor the self while serving others.

After all, her words are meant for others.

WRESTLING WITH WORDS

By Dr. Rona Thau

As a teen and young adult, journaling and writing poems and songs kept me sane. They were my staple go-to's for comfort and guidance. It was through my writing that I touched the direct experience of an intuitive knowledge far more vast than my mind. Finding this connection provided me with comfort and an infinitely powerful source of fuel.

During these mystical writing interludes, I questioned, spoke freely, and felt swept up in spontaneous insights. Words worked their way through me, using me as a conduit to freely deliver spiritual knowledge from a higher source. Writing steered me through and out of conflicts and confusion. My curiosity drew me closer to this wisdom. It harmonized my soul.

But all of this changed during my last year or two of high school English composition, and grew worse during college. I struggled to write. Things that were meaningful became trapped in a framework of arbitrary writing rules. As a result, my writing, my joy, and my creativity began to weaken, deteriorate, and outright fail. How could I actually believe there was only one way to express things correctly? To formulate a poem? To speak from the heart? Suddenly, I was being taught that my natural love of spontaneous creative writing was wrong. And worse, I believed it. My writing was imperfect. I was issued Ds and, around that time, my spirit broke. Cracked.

Saddened, I set my writing aside for a long while, somehow

afraid I might be of harm, not understanding the silly rules, I abandoned what had always brought me a sense of comfort, peace, and inner knowing.

I don't recommend you do that, ever.

Instead of remembering how freeing writing could be, and how valuable it had proven as a means working things through my mind, I suited myself with armor, and with others' unflattering opinions. And because I let go of what allowed me to truly grasp hold of my life path, it became an ugly struggle. Because I believed others were "right" and I was "wrong," I created much misery for myself by essentially banning myself from the writing arena. Even worse, I banned myself from myself.

If and when I did write, it felt more like an argument with myself than what it used to be: a lesson from a wise teacher, a soothing voice of guidance from a source that connected and grounded me; a continuous flow that opened me up.

I felt so lost without that light at my helm. Instead of writing to ease and free my soul, as I once had, I wrote to try to please. I contorted into a mold I didn't fit. A choke hold squeezed my voice silent. Sad.

Simple trip-ups created an inner affect that swept my soul roots from beneath me. All the things that writing used to nurture in me now weighed me down. For this reason, I simply let it go. I pulled the plug and gave it up. Why? Because I gave others the power to be "right" and further allowed that to make me, in turn, "wrong."

Wrong choice.

I finally realized that my drive to question life by writing was necessary. My voice, like yours, needs a venue. Writing can lead us—and our readers—to hidden treasures that would otherwise remain locked away. You can evoke a deep awareness through your writing, whether it's with prose, poems, or fairy tales. But if your self-awareness turns into a virulent critic, just pivot to get a clearer outlook.

Writing can be the greatest gift. A crafty tool to unwind life's useful lessons.

Let it unwrap You.

I wish I had seen sooner that by distrusting my instincts, I put myself in a dangerous position. I pinned and pummeled myself into a pitiful pulp. I surrendered when I needed to stand and keep kicking. Not to be right, but to be me as best as I could be.

I abandoned myself and left the ring, tail between legs, feeling both wrong and worthless.

Self-doubt and judgment left unchecked is a rabid killer. A Life-Spirit killer. Don't do that. I missed mingling with the rhymes that had once riddled through me. Something within urged a reunion. Now, I allow that sense of something I feel to move through me. A muse or a mystic... call it what you will.

It's unseen, forceful, graceful, giddy, and light. It spans wider than the horizon. It hums and drums deliberately. I love feeling connected to whatever it is and respect Its authority over any old set of "rules" as ultimate guidance. Source.

Wrestling with your writing is worthwhile. Writing presents space for playfulness, peacefulness, or even a battlefield to blaze through troubles we wrestle with. It needs us to let it out. Its creation should remain unencumbered by "rules" that seek to keep it stuck or bound. Let it flow through you. Transcend.

There will be times when you wrestle with the words. Allow for fresh opportunity if you feel bound or stuck. Take a walk, listen to music, dance, delve into a book, workout, meditate—do something to unstick.

The words need you to write.

Dr. Rona Thau *believes that life's most valuable asset is inner happiness, and has since her earliest memories. Rona has evolved as a spiritual creative, yogi, health doctor, and food lover, and is pioneering an Ageless Living Revolution as a way to connect people to inner happiness through food, movement, and mindset. Ageless Living lets you feel, function, and be free successfully. It's necessary now. We all deserve to be happy and free. As ageless living techniques catch on, the movement will be swift. It's a fun path. Connect with Rona at DrRonaThau.com.*

MAYBE YOU SHOULD QUIT

By Joshua Harbert

It's the day before a deadline, and the writing isn't going well. I reread everything I've written so far. A handful of half-starts to various thoughts and ideas litter the page. My writing feels jumbled. The sentences don't flow. I don't feel like using any of it.

Ten minutes pass. Twenty minutes pass. Half an hour passes. I start wondering,

> *"What makes you think you're a writer? Why don't you just give up and do something else? Why don't you pick a different path?"*

The doubts aren't new. The questions have echoed through my head over the last several weeks and months. I'm starting to wonder if they're speaking the truth. Maybe the voice inside my head is right. Maybe I should just give up.

Frustrated, I go complain to my wife, telling her I'm not a good writer and that I want to quit. She listens to my story. But instead of offering advice or encouragement, she asks a single question: "Why don't you just stop writing?"

There it is. I have permission to go either way. There's no pressure—just a simple yes or no. And in the face of so clear a choice, I know what to do. As much as I feel like quitting, something inside won't let me. So I decide to keep writing.

Maybe you're facing similar doubts. Maybe you're questioning whether you should keep traveling along this path of writing. Maybe you're wondering if it's still worth doing.

There's much I could say to encourage you. I could tell you how writing lets you touch people deeply—how you can speak directly to their hearts and minds, how you can move them to meaningful action, and how you can leave them better than you found them. I could tell you how writing enables you to uncover and communicate truth—about the world, others, and yourself. I could tell you how writing gives us the chance to forge community and connection with like-minded people. I could tell you writing offers an opportunity to express who you are to the world, and to be seen by others.

But although each of these are true, the simple reality is that they won't be helpful to you at this moment.

First of all, you've probably heard them all already. And you've even experienced them for yourself at some point or another. So expanding on them isn't going to cover any new ground. Second of all, and more importantly, you can find the same benefits in other places. Photography, business, physics, finance, philosophy, engineering, and countless other fields offer similar opportunities for self-discovery, growth, and impact. Who am I to say that another craft wouldn't suit you better?

Instead, I'm going to give you permission to quit. If you feel writing isn't working out for you, feel free to drop it. Feel free to explore something else. Feel free to try something different.

I know that you're thoughtful and wise. I know you'll succeed and thrive on whatever path you take. I know that you'll make the choice that's best for you. All I ask is that you decide one way or another. Commit one hundred percent. Your life is too valuable—and you have too much to offer the world—to live halfway.

So what will it be? Do you want to take another path? Or do you want to keep writing? The choice is yours.

Joshua Harbert *helps people weave meaning and compassion into everyday moments. In 14 years growing up in Kenya, he witnessed the beauty and grace of humanity amid the injustices of poverty. Efforts to live, and help others live, into that humanity drive much of his thinking and writing. Specifically, he serves people on a mission by crafting action-generating copy and by sharing weekly stories/wisdom at The Bright Army. When he's not writing, you can find him wandering the neighborhoods of Chicago, training in Taekwondo, playing with his wife and daughter, or smiling at a squirrel.*

WRITE TO CREATE YOUR OWN MIRROR

By Jean Powell

You know that feeling you get when someone is about to see you naked for the first time? Just the idea of it makes me want to run and hide.

I envision the scar from when I fell down running in heels in the rain. The fading marks from being eaten alive by mosquitoes on a trip to India. The inevitable bruise I have on my knee because it seems I always have one. They are parts of my past, but the flaws are still visible. I want to pull the sheet over me and wrap it around me a hundred times.

Judgmentally, I define my body as imperfect. I ruthlessly think: Why did I stop running? Those cookies were unnecessary. I wish I didn't like beer so much. Sitting in the sun a bit wouldn't have hurt. Completely exposed, every fault feels spotlighted. Closing my eyes, I pretend they aren't there. I desperately want to pull every shade and remove every bit of light.

As I enter into the world of published writing, that familiar, naked discomfort floods through me. I've unveiled an intimate part of myself, something I created while sitting alone in contemplation in the safety of my room. All of my fears, inadequacies, and insecurities scream in bold font under the magnifying glass of the world.

In other sectors of my life, I easily share publicly. I give speeches at events. I post on social media regularly. I upload my pretend artistic photos to Instagram. I tweet whenever it feels right.In this curated world, we have the ability to carefully piece together the perfect costume for show: Hey, look at this cool place I'm at… See me having fun with my awesome friends… I can quote something thought-provoking.

We add a flattering filter; we airbrush. We build our highlight reel to be just that. The shiny moments we want the world to see. While spotlighting our expertise or re-taking our photo 10 times, we mask any vulnerabilities or imperfections. And then we habitually check our phones to see if there are enough likes, shares and ReTweets to validate us.

Amidst all of our self-editing, we stop being able to fully see ourselves. We become wrapped up in our new, custom-manufactured identity, absorbing it as our own. We begin to believe the retouched image is the original.

Writing forces you to examine yourself, uncloaking intimacies and showing glimpses of previously unseen places. When you allow the words to pour out, writing sends an invitation to the world for a grand public viewing, prompting those who have known you to take a deeper look at those things within you that were previously tagged exclusive.

For the first few months after I started writing my own blog, I didn't share any of my posts. I kept my website intentionally hidden and, beyond my fellow writers and a few others (most of whom had only known me for a couple months at best), I kept this world concealed. Instead of running around in exhibitionism, blogging made me want to wear winter coats, scarves, and boots. It was as though I was standing on stage in a large coliseum, flawed and nude, while everyone scrutinized every detail and judged me. I wanted to cling to my edit mode, furiously hit my delete button, beat down the inner voice asking me to write, and tell it no.

I would be lying by omission if I didn't say I quit a few

times. There have been times when I wanted to burn it all down, delete every post, and liberate my URL.

But the longer I denied the voice, the more the words pushed and flowed upward again. The desire to express tormented me, causing sessions of soul-searching and internal interrogations. The messages and stories wanted to be set free. My soul ached to be seen.

So I undid the tightly knotted belt and threw off the robe. I picked a day, closed my eyes, and shared my written heart with the world. Bracing for impact, I lay awake all night in anxious nervousness, occasionally glancing at the phone I didn't want to check. As I picked it up and began to sift through the notifications and messages, my heart beat wildly.

This is me, and I'm posting my nudes in public. Flinch.

And then, this deliciously surprising and overwhelming thing happened. People read my pieces. They wanted to read more. My words helped them identify with their own fears and desires, encouraging them to look deeper and articulate their own. They let my experiences inspire them and encountered unexpected lessons. They found themselves in my stories.

I found others were starving for this level of shared identity. We made eye contact through our souls. I discovered connection on an intimate level I had never before found, often with people I had never met.

Writing is creating our own mirror so we can take an honest look inside. The self-made façade is forced to fade away, and is replaced with an authentic reflection of our truest selves. Gleaming back at us, we find our fueled beliefs, suppressed desires, and quiet dreams. The seemingly sexy stories we've told ourselves are stripped away to reveal our delicate hearts. We uncover weaknesses, pain, and heartache in a way that allows us to explore them and their origins. We learn ourselves.

Seeing yourself so clearly is not easy. Writing forces you to sit in those dark places you deny, confronting the ugliness, turning off the filtration system, and leaving parts of you raw. There are plenty of times I just want to lock away my laptop.

But a writer's gift is self-discovery, in which accelerated learning and growth are inevitable. We walk about life hyperaware, waiting to encounter the next lesson to be explored, extracted, and shared. We experience the fulfillment that comes from creation, from connecting the dots in our own lives to those in others.

Once you've identified with the reflection shining back at you, writing propels you to dig deeper. You cultivate the topsoil, proud of the new earth you've uprooted, only to find there are many more layers, some you weren't aware existed. You make new discoveries, unearth new questions, and encounter a new level of awareness.

I realized I wanted to know more of what I had to say, what I could root up, what messages lay untouched at my core. Expressing this level of myself, I found a new connection with others. And by allowing them to see my willingness to share my imperfections, I inspired them to join me and be free.

I am still learning how to be naked. I still fight the urge to drown myself in an oversized hoodie and look away. But each scar I unveil allows me discover myself more wholly and share.

Explore what your mirror has to reveal. Your reflection has beautiful and honest truths that await.

Jean Powell is the Director of Sales for Taphandles brewery marketing and is currently building a new beer branding agency. She believes sales to be the most powerful vehicle to grow personally and accelerate the development of those around her. Jean teaches the necessity and awesomeness of selling in everyday life, removing the fear and blocks from rejection and confrontation. Her desire is to revolutionize how managers lead teams, focusing on culture over strategy and heart over head. Jean is currently developing sales/sales management content and resources. Get updates and read more from her at JeanOnTap.com and on Twitter @JeanOnTap.

WRITING: THE LAST GREAT FORM
OF SELF-EXPRESSION

By Tom Meitner

For your own mental and emotional health, you need to find a way to express yourself. Self-expression is actually a really valuable form of therapy. And yet, it's all too easy to slip into the same traps that everyone has fallen into for decades, to become a part of the herd. Go for a walk around a mall sometime and you'll see it.

The hipster—striving for individuality—wears thick black frames, some form of ironic facial hair, and jeans in a size that would be my own version of hell (give me some room!). The punk / emo / whatever chick with funny-colored hair (probably shaved on one side of her head, because that's a thing now)— aiming for unique—wears something black, and has various pieces of metal stuck in her face and body, seen and unseen.

You get the idea. Somebody young-ish tries to express themselves but, in reality, they're just saying "Hey, I'm part of [insert group here]."

It happens in so many different areas of life. Many people who want to express themselves in music wind up playing cover songs on YouTube, thinking they are expressing something deep about themselves. But they're not: they're just along for the ride.

It's easy to copy. I do it all the time. A good 80 to 90 percent of my daily conversation consists of quotes from funny TV shows and awesome movies from the '80s and '90s. There's nothing wrong with that.

But I never feel more honest than when I'm sitting down with a blank document in front of me. When it's just me and the writing. That honesty clears my head, keeps me grounded, and can pull me through whatever emotional funk I'm going through.

Sure, I can rip off the tone of Hemingway. I can write in the style of Sylvia Plath. That's all good, and wouldn't necessarily be wrong. But the words—the meat of what I'm writing—still have to come from me.

As a result, what's left on the page is pure, unadulterated me.

It's not always pretty, but that's okay. Neither am I. It's not always funny or insightful. But whatever it is, it's me. It's a snapshot of myself. A little glimpse into my brain at the moment the pen hit the paper or my fingers hit the keys.

Expressing yourself isn't just something you do to get noticed. It's something you can do to explore your own brain, and to un-stick yourself when you need it most.

How often do you find yourself stuck? It can happen in any number of ways:

- Developing an idea at work
- Struggling with a personal weakness
- Striving to reach a goal
- Battling through a relationship problem

...and so on. These are problems every one of us can go through. But often, the problem lies not in the situation itself, but in how you react to it. At the risk of sounding a little zen-ish, the problem lies within you.

That may not be something you want to admit to yourself. But the cool part of realizing you're the problem is that you now have the control. You can fix the problem.

One of the best ways I have to work through problems is by

dumping everything that's kicking around in my brain out onto a sheet of paper or onto a computer screen. That's right, kids: free writing isn't just something your teachers made you do in school because they ran out of productive work to give you. It's a unique tool that lets you express what you're thinking and feeling.

Here's how it works: Shut everything down. Close the door. Silence your phone. Open up a blank Word document, or grab a notebook and a pen. Now, for 10 minutes, just write. Anything. Everything. Whatever pops into your mind, get it out onto the page. No editing. No revising. No judgment.

It'll be a struggle. I have a beast of an internal editor who is always re-reading as I type, correcting little goofball mistakes here and there. I have to beat him into submission when I free write.

But you know what ends up on the page at the end of 10 minutes?

Me.

I'm right there. My hopes, my fears, my problems and, often, my solutions. It's not a satire. It's not a parody. It's not copying. It's just you.

If you want to express yourself openly and honestly to yourself and others, just write. It's the simplest, cheapest, and easiest form of self-expression. Plus, it's a lot less painful than all those piercings.

Tom Meitner is an author and copywriter living in Milwaukee, WI. After receiving his English degree and having zero direction in his life, he stumbled upon a book about freelance writing. Since then, he hasn't looked back, and has been happily freelancing and building businesses since the spring of 2008. You can usually find him hanging out at TomMeitner.com.

Write to See the Miracles around You

By Jennifer Price

I was standing on the shore when the water suddenly engulfed me in a biting tide. I remember looking up at a sky full of lightning, with a mass of dark clouds thick and looming above me. Rain poured out and the current began swirling, taking people and debris and me with it. Like a giant water tornado, it lifted me with huge force, and then I felt it pulling me under as I spun around. Choking, convinced I wouldn't make it, I gulped for air. Suddenly, the storm's fury jarred me awake and realized I was at home, in my bed. Relief swept through my limbs. Death had never seemed so close and inescapable.

Pretty sure there would be no more sleep in my near future, I shoved my feet out of bed for an early morning run. Fear from the dream still had me reeling, and my fingers were shaking as I tied my shoes, eager to get my muscles moving to work out the residual anxiety.

About a mile into my route, Seal's "Love's Divine" began to play on my iPod. The song's sound effects and lyrics were too much to be a coincidence: "Then the rainstorm came, over me... I need love to help me know my name."

I was a little freaked out. I knew it was some sort of message sent for me, something I was supposed to understand. As soon as I returned home, I opened up my laptop and began to transcribe my thoughts onto the screen.

I described how frightened I had been, how real the storm

had felt, how it all appeared out of nowhere. Then I scratched out the many ways the song lyrics could explain my dream. Tears fell as I found the words and realized the clear meaning: I was drowning.

Not just in my dream.

I was drowning because I was not expressing myself. I was not sharing my emotions with the people in my life who were closest to me. I suddenly understood that writing could be the form of expression I needed.

I soon found that, the more I wrote, the more I noticed the synchronicities and miracles all around me, staring me in the face. The simplest conversations with friends had so much more significance because I recognized links to other apparently unimportant moments of my day. Dragonflies and leaves on trees whispered to me in a language I hadn't understood before. I heard my daughter sing and change song lyrics with new messages I'm sure were sent by angels.

It happened again and again, and I found myself delighted at the continual surprise of unexplained incidents leaving important clues for me to discover. Writing about them helped me decipher the clues, so I could make sense out of the wonder.

Writing has helped me see the little bits of myself I might not have seen otherwise, that I sometimes don't even realize are hiding somewhere inside me until I'm writing them down. The smallest details and most beautiful moments are revealed through my writing. They reach out, offering direction and guiding me to where my heart wants to go.

There was a tiny, brief millisecond when I doubted myself, and wondered if I was assigning meaning to things that didn't really have any. Was I making it all up for my own amusement? Then I realized I had to trust myself, that I was reading the cues correctly, that they were indeed connected and were placed there to show me the way.

Besides, it really makes no difference which signs are real and which are imagined. Either way, my interpretations of them gave me new awareness of my world, of myself.

This awareness brings joy and awe to the mundane, weight to every letter on the page. My mind, heart, and soul show themselves slowly as I unfold the mysteries in myself with each word. I begin to understand my dreams.

Once you start to write about your dreams and ideas, they start to happen. And that is the miracle of writing. Writing is a miracle that makes dreams come true.

Jennifer Price is a copywriter who touches hearts and minds with words that give a graceful caress, a gentle nudge, and an oh-so-sweet feeling that inevitably leads to a "YES." She's a dreamteller who helps creative business owners express and realize their vision, bringing it to life with words. Jennifer's strong experience as a marketing and sales executive enables her to incite emotional response and allure loyal enthusiasts to unique brands. Jennifer is online at YouSoMuch.com.

A Love Letter to Writing

By Clare Herbert

I love to write. I love the physicality of writing. The tip-tap of my fingers on the keyboard, the slow draw of a pen across a page, the feel of a clean piece of paper. I feel most like me when I have a pen in my hand.

I love the process of translating my thoughts into a series of lines and shapes on a page. I love the power and precision of the perfect word in the perfect sentence. I love how a reader can absorb and interpret my words in their own way. It's an amazingly intimate process, between writer and reader. My thoughts and ideas get uploaded into someone else's world.

I write to understand the world. I never really know what I think about a topic until I've written about it. Each piece is a collection of ideas. A snapshot of where I am in time today, a souvenir. I write to find my place, to untangle the mass of thoughts in my mind. Writing often feels like I am literally pouring my heart and mind out. I just pick up my soul, tip it over slowly, and pour it out, like pouring milk from a jug. I write to impose order on internal chaos. Molding words into linear patterns creates a sense of calm. I spill out my ideas and make sense of them on the page. I write for companionship, connection, and understanding. I write to be helpful, kind, and creative. I feel like a member of the human race when I write.

I write to understand my own story. I write to know how I feel, how it all connects and why it matters. I write letters to people I love.

For years, I didn't write. It was too painful and revelatory. My expectations were too high. It felt daunting and totally overwhelming.

Slowly, over the years, I grew into it. I began writing more and more. It became a habit, a daily practice based on the power of showing up and doing the work regardless of the outcome. Today, I'd be lost without my journal.

I love reading about other writers' rituals. I love the journey writing takes from a fleeting abstract thought through a number of iterations before it arrives neatly packaged, tightly worded, and ready to be published. Writing is a career that elicits awe in people, which always amuses me. There's little of that reverence in the simple practice of putting your bum in the chair and writing for hours on end. It's a graft, as well as a craft. It's about practice and showing up.

Every writer does it differently. But this is how I do it:

- I write a lot. I fill a journal every month. I aim to publish a couple of times a week. I write as part of my work as a journalist and consultant.

- I write in cheap, A4 spiral notebooks. Fancy journals make me seize up with the pressure of having to write something mind-blowing. Loose-leaf pages make me feel chaotic. I use cheap ballpoint pens in blue or black, often freebies from hotels and product launches.

- I write everywhere. On the bus, in bed, in the bath. No matter where I am in the world, it's just me, my thoughts, and my pen. It's tremendously comforting.

- I write on a single blank page. I pour it all out until my mind is free of it. I end up with a huge, amorphous, repetitive blob of words. I aim to get it on the page without wondering how or why or what. In my head, it's chaotic, contradictory, and weird. Once there are words on the page, I can work with them.

- I hunt for the thread that holds it all together: the lesson I want to teach, the idea I want to share, the reaction I want to elicit.

- I chip away at the chaos until I feel it come together. I mold it until each idea fits and flows.

- Most of my work starts life as a fleeting thought captured in my journal. I jot things down, connect them, move them around like toy soldiers on a battlefield. I doodle. I draw shapes and maps and squiggles.

- Writing is woven into my day, from my morning pages in bed to a handwritten to-do list to hours tip-tapping on my laptop. I do it without realizing.

- Some pieces are written quickly, in one sitting, when a particular thought just needs to come out. Others are slow, laborious efforts molded and edited over weeks. (This piece falls into the latter category.)

- I need white space when I write. My desk is ridiculously simple (pens, papers, candle, and water); the walls are bare. I close my browser and try to keep it closed. I focus on the blank page.

- I keep a list of random thoughts as I write. I like to capture all the distractions that bubble up. Often, there's good stuff in there. Capturing it allows me to keep my focus on what I want to say now. I give my ideas homes so I can go back and visit them later.

- I keep a list of article ideas. There are ideas that have been there for more than five years, which I'll likely never use. I have piles of unfinished articles, half-thoughts, and vague ideas.

- I love and crave long, free, empty periods of time for writing. I love diving into the big ideas and getting lost, resurfacing for food after hours immersed. I love writing furiously, trying to keep up with my thoughts. I love the sense of peace that comes after the idea is out there. I feel unburdened, as if I've done my part of the bargain.

- I don't permit writers block. I simply don't allow it. I see writing as my job and treat it with the professionalism it deserves. If the words aren't coming, I stop. Rather than torment myself, I take a break. Something physical or repetitive usually gets me going again. Yoga, hoovering, laundry—something that requires my focus so I can't dwell on the issue. I try not to get lost wandering the Internet in procrastination. I'm trying to develop that focus muscle.

I do all this work with one goal in mind. *"The happiest man alive would look in the mirror and see himself exactly as he is,"* says Dumbledore to Harry Potter in The Sorcerer's Stone. I want my writing to feel like me, to sound like me, to mirror me.

That's my goal.

Clare Herbert is a writer, career strategist, and social entrepreneur currently based in Dublin, Ireland. Her writing has been featured in a number of national publications including The Irish Times and The Sunday Times. As an entrepreneurial journalist, Clare has appeared on live national television and radio, and has spoken at a number of international conferences. Clare spent 10 years working in the non-profit sector across four continents, from Washington, D.C., to India to rural Zambia. Clare currently works as a career strategist supporting activists, change-makers, and social entrepreneurs, helping them build meaningful and impactful careers. Find her online at ClareHerbert.com.

29

By Stephanie Jiroch

It took 29 years before I called myself a writer. Twenty-nine years I dabbled in the art of the written word. Twenty-nine years I spent playing with the order and understanding of sentences to elicit emotion. Twenty-nine years to own my value as a master of the written word.

My first memories are of writing. Scribbles upon scribbles covered my grandmother's yellow legal notepads, purchased by her in bulk after she discovered my obsession with storytelling at the tender age of 2. By 8, I was writing full fiction, ad copy, and poetry from the sun-soaked wooden floor of the tree house my grandfather had lovingly built before his untimely death. I carried within me the stories brought by the wind from far-off places I had only read about in my books.

I wrote daily. I wrote in journals, in class, and in my free time. I wrote award-winning essays in high school, academic papers in college and, then, I stopped. I stopped the tales of love and hope, the stories of good and evil. My well of inspiration dried up. My witty taglines lost their spark.

The years that followed were dark, except for my journals, as I navigated the waters of another beast: grief.

The loss of my mother left me confused and blind in a dark world that the safety net of my words couldn't reach. There was no baby blanket for my sadness. No book that could bring her back. No words that could express my anguish, my fears, my deep pit of loneliness. There was nothing to say and, for once, my pen ran dry and the clean pages of my notepads went untouched.

I quit not out of resistance, not out of choice, but from the tsunami effect of my emotions that washed forth from my heart and into my life.

And then, as it always seems to, a season of new life nudged itself awake with the first blossoms of hope. And just like that, the season of grief had run its course.

With renewed optimism and a touch of unexpected joy, I reached for what I knew: my pen. Within that moment, my muse resumed her work and, just as Sleeping Beauty rose from that first kiss, so did my first stories, rising from that deep dark place that only I had known for far too long.

The words poured out like a favorite song on a hot summer night, getting louder and louder as you sing the tune that makes you feel more alive than ever before. The sorrow, the grief, the fears no longer defined me. Whether I wrote or not was no longer at the whim of my emotions and, at the tender age of 29, I took the bold stand of owning the title, Writer.

It is what I've always done. It is what I will always do. It pours forth from my soul through the grief and the joy, the ups and the downs, and the rollercoaster that we call Life.

The idea of quitting no longer held me in her ironclad clutches. The idea that my words didn't matter no longer had merit. The creativity that once cowered in the corner had finally come out in all her glory. And in the moments when I question if I should continue, I simply remember:

"My time here is limited.
I will not die with the stories in my heart untold.
My voice will not go unheard.
I will not die without giving it my all."

Stephanie Jiroch is empowering women to live fun and fabulous lives by flirting with all that life has to offer. As the founder of Flirt With Life℠, Stephanie teaches women all over the world how to manifest their truest desires so they can start living their dream life without fear and with ease. She has spent the last six years working with women to enhance their lives physically, mentally, and emotionally as a coach, yoga instructor, and holistic health practitioner. Connect with her on Twitter @StephanieJiroch and visit StephanieJiroch.com for more ways to flirt with life.

THE FLOURISHING WRITER:
CONCLUDING THOUGHTS

By Dave Ursillo

The Flourishing Writer is no longer motivated to prove anything, garnish respect, or change the opinions of dissenters. As The Flourishing Writer, you're no longer writing to appease others but flexing your heart as a conduit and proponent of love. You're no longer producing content as if on a factory line, but producing high-quality, idea-moving, world-changing testaments that reflect beauty, depth, and your unrelenting calling to embrace this life for all that it is, so that others like you may do the same.

Thus, flourishing dawns at the creative crossroads of "the self and others"—a place where the synthesis of need and desire can combine to infuse your personal motivations (your artistic desire, creative explorations, and high personal standards) with a deep desire to give, inspire, empower, lead, and serve other human beings.

Flourishing is a place where these personal desires complement and empower you to a higher level of artistic creation: the art gets better and better, and the mission behind the art reaches the eyes and hearts of others more and more. As the Flourishing Writer, raw passion is replaced by mission and the purpose behind the art takes center stage. The message is for those who need it, and both the high praise of fans and the dissenting criticism of disbelievers is cast aside for what it is: unimportant, distracting noise.

Whether the purpose behind your art involves making the world a better place, influencing socio-political change, teaching, sharing through story, educating children, or something else entirely, as a Flourishing Writer, you create work that serves your guiding values and personal beliefs while also serving others.

What drives the writing goes far beyond ordinary self-expression. Rather, it carries the weight of intentional mission: to communicate ideas, to explore dilemmas, to open hearts, to be a mirror that shines back to those reading eyes a greater depth of knowledge, understanding, and awareness.

And that is the mission I wish to impart upon you with these final words, friend.

Your writing journey is bound to be a long one: no matter who you are, your creative journey will be full of many trials and obstacles—and just as rewards and pleasures.

But that is the point.

Your creative journey is no different than your life's journey.

You will find correlation after correlation; similarity after similarity. The creative life you live as a writer will help to teach you, inspire you and open up your heart throughout every step of your life as a human being who wishes to craft a lasting legacy of love in the words you sow and the goodness you share with others.

So, you really can't quit writing, friend. You have too much life to live. Too many beautiful moments to experience. Too many trials to triumph over. And too much love to share.

And it's writing that will show you the way.

RESOURCES

For Writers of All Levels

Clare's Ten Rules for Writing

by Clare Herbert

1. Do your morning pages: write three pages longhand every morning before you do anything else.

2. Write on a computer that isn't connected to the Internet. Regularly disconnect from the virtual world and go lie under a tree.

3. When in doubt, choose to live a life worth writing about.

4. Keep a notebook, computer file, or Tumblr for "random thoughts." Track the ideas that occur to you, the idiosyncrasies that strike you, the themes that light you up. Give each idea a home so you can come back and visit them later.

5. Read widely and often.

6. Don't overcomplicate it. Sit down and write. Don't edit; just write.

7. Give yourself a deadline. Raise the bar on your work. Be prolific.

8. Experiment with writing via different tools. Coloring, writing by hand, typing, scrawling in the bath, working at a desk. Experiment.

9. Don't get mad; get curious. If your writing feels stuck or rigid, ask why. Write about that.

10. Write every day.

TEN THINGS EVERY WRITER MUST REMEMBER

by Tom Meitner

1. We live in an unprecedented era where writers can build audiences, careers, and lifestyles with a few clicks of the mouse.

2. I'm constantly amazed at how much power we hold in our hands, in our homes and offices, just by sitting in front of a computer screen.

3. You can be the best writer in the world but, if you can't get people to notice you, you'll just be writing to yourself.

4. Unless you're really good at it, don't try to be funny when you write. Let it come naturally. If you sit down to "be funny," it'll be forced and painful.

5. You have a unique voice in there somewhere, but the only way to find it is to keep writing. Give it a chance to come out.

6. Sometimes, the best therapy in the world is just a piece of paper and a pen.

7. Everything you enjoy, everything that moves you, everything that convinces you to take action... it all starts with words that somebody wrote.

8. Can anybody be a writer? Sure. But the difference between a writer and a great writer is showing up every day to write. A writer writes whenever they feel like it. A great writer

writes—period.

9. Even the tiniest pieces of life can spark a piece of writing. Start viewing the world around you as a wealth of possibilities and ideas.

10. You don't "try" to be a writer. You either write or you don't. If you write, start calling yourself a writer. Respect yourself and that title and you'll be surprised at the progress you make.

TAKE AN INSPIRATION SAFARI

by Clare Herbert

When you don't know what to write about, take an inspiration safari. Visit the following locations:

- Lie on the ground, watching the expanse of sky change.
- Go be in water: take a shower, soak in the tub, visit the ocean.
- Have a cup of coffee, a glass of red wine, some nice, dark chocolate.
- Dance. Dark room + loud music = liberation.
- Develop writing rituals. I like vanilla candles, pints of cold water, bright rooms, and silence. Find an array of scents, sounds, and textures to prompt your writing.
- Immerse yourself in something physical and methodical, like cooking or laundry. Give your brain a chance to find a new rhythm.
- Create a daily writing practice. Be it morning pages, a gratitude list before bed, or a 500-word exploration of a topic every day.
- Write a letter to someone you love, to someone who inspires you, to someone you want to know.
- Write about what pisses you off.
- Start today. Like, right now. Set a timer for 20 minutes. Write.

AUTHOR AFFIRMATIONS

"Simplicity is an art, as is complexity."

— JOE CHOI

"Let your mission shine through regardless of the deadlines,
dead ends, and droughts."

— MEGAN ATKINSON

"Our imaginations are linked by the cyclical act
of writing and reading."

— CAITLIN WALSH

"Stay connected to your heart.
It's where your inspiration and integrity lie."

— LORI MANCINI

"If it weren't for those positive people in my life who brought me back up out of the darkness and spoke life over me, I never would have fallen in love with words, writing, life, and me again. People have the power to speak life into your life, even during those pitch-black times, but you have to choose to hear the words.

"If you don't have a friend like this, I'll be that friend for you. I'll sing loving words to you because you need to know just how precious you are and how valuable your story is."

— DIANE PAULEY

"When the writing gets tough, the tough get writing."

— JASON VANFOSSON

"Why aren't you a writer? It's a fear of being less-than-perfect when presenting to the world."

— AMY OUELLETTE

"When you write, you are unearthing yourself."

— DAVE URSILLO

"Great writing is just a way of speaking the truth. If you don't want to write today, you're probably afraid of the truth."

— MILO McLAUGHLIN

"Fear is what makes it exciting."

— CASSIA COGGER

"Your desire to write continues to burn,
no matter how tired you feel."

— LISA LANDTROOP

"Being a writer allows us to lure out our subconscious, to bring it
into the light and to feed it. Writing allows us to stretch our
beings and live through the characters,
we bring to life on the page."

— JESSICA GLENDINNING

"The best books are the books that weren't written for money,
but out of passion and desire."

— LAURYN DOLL

"Allow your thoughts to run free."

— SANG THI DUONG

"I must write because there are millions and millions of words
hidden in my head and within the crevices of my heart, yearning
to be heard, to be seen, to encourage and to empower."

— KADENA TATE

"Writing doesn't have limits or walls unless I create them."
— MEAGAN CHRISTINE WILLIAMS

"Buckle negative self-judgment in the back seat. Distract it with a toy, and keep yourself safe by focusing on the road ahead."
— Dr. RONA THAU

"Who am I to say that another craft wouldn't suit you better?"
— JOSHUA HARBERT

"I need to write. To explore myself. To see what sticks. To decide what makes my heart beat. To be accountable to getting better. To find other members of my tribe who align with my internal values. To find those who argue and oppose to decide whether I will defend my beliefs and contemplate their strength.
To explore the depths of my thoughts
and learn the inner part of my soul.

"Because this discomfort is why I started in the first place. Because stretching and pushing myself is how I take it to the next level. Because this feeling doesn't just go away. Because it's how I open new opportunities. Because my heart has a message that wants to come out. Because I wanted to quit and need to write my comeback story. Because this is what I'd tell someone else to do."
— JEAN POWELL

"What's left on the page is pure, unadulterated me."

— TOM MEITNER

"The more you write, the more you will uncover
the mysteries in yourself."

— JENNIFER PRICE

"I want my writing to feel like me,
to sound like me, to mirror me."

— CLARE HERBERT

"My words matter. My stories matter. What I offer up in my
life's purpose is perspective, inspiration, and hope
through the written word."

— STEPHANIE JIROCH

ABOUT THE AUTHORS

ABOUT DAVE URSILLO

Dave Ursillo Jr. is a multi-published author and creative entrepreneur who founded *The Literati Writers*ˢᴹ in 2012. *The Literati Writers*ˢᴹ is a premium-membership online writing community that was created to provide a uniquely supportive and safe space where like-minded writers from around the world could unite to share their creative journeys alongside supportive peers. As an online support system, this writers' group exists to help writers of all levels make life's journey all the more rewarding, every step of the way.

Dave is the author of *God Whispers on the Wind* (July 2012) and *Lead Without Followers* (September 2011), and has contributed to five other books. He has been featured on CBS News Sunday Morning, *Chicken Soup for the Soul*, Inc.com, and Zen Habits, and is a member of The Young Entrepreneur Council. This book is the first collaborative project championed by *The Literati Writers*ˢᴹ with many more to come.

Afflicted with sporadic wanderlust, Dave finds himself a former resident of New York City's East Village, Washington, D.C., and Boston, Massachusetts. He is spending 2013 traveling to new destinations across two continents, including the Hawaiian Islands, Northern Europe, and British Columbia. Dave plans to continue writing in ink, energy, and smiles upon the street—wherever his travels might take him. Find out more about Dave and *The Literati Writers*ˢᴹ at LiteratiWriters.com.

ABOUT THE LITERATI WRITERS℠

The Literati Writers℠ is a premium-membership online writers' group for writers who understand the importance of community support, high level learning opportunities and accountability to make their writing dreams a reality. Founded by multi-published author and creative entrepreneur Dave Ursillo in 2012, *The Literati Writers*℠ is a uniquely supportive writing community featuring dozens of writers from more than seven countries who want to live and love their creative journeys, every step of the way.

The Literati Writers℠ is the ideal support system for an independent entrepreneur, aspiring author or self-employed creative who understands the need for a whole new level of investment, commitment, accountability and growth to flourish in his or her life. We provide exactly that.

Featuring a private discussion forum for idea-generation, intelligent conversation and setting weekly accountability goals, members of The Literati Writers℠ also receive priceless personal support and learning opportunities through regular group conference calls with the community, speaking to published authors and entrepreneurs every month in live interviews, receiving original curriculum by email every week from Literati founder Dave Ursillo, and much more. Visit LiteratiWriters.com/Apply to submit your membership application today.

MEET THE AUTHORS

Megan Atkinson is the Chief Word Nerd at Ignite Your Cause, where doing good and doing business are not mutually exclusive. She's merged the artistry of the written word with her philanthropic tendencies to help nonprofits and social entrepreneurs inspire the masses, influence change, and infuse more good into the world. When she's not writing for a cause, she works with solopreneurs to devise sizzling give-back action plans that bolster their brands and deliver the warm-fuzzies. To infuse a dash of do-goodery into the work you do, visit IgniteYourCause.com.

Joe Choi is a direct response copywriter for the health market. He usually tries something completely new every two years just to shake things up. Through all these shake-ups, his addiction to golf, yoga, avocados, tuna cooked rare, donuts, and beef jerky have remained the same. You can find him at his local golf course or yoga studio, or writing about a bunch of things at FescueFairways.com. Follow him on Twitter @jchoi007.

Jeanine Nicole Cerundolo is a writer, certified yoga instructor, and trained group coaching facilitator who facilitates transformation in people's lives. Through her experience with social work and education, coupled with a passion for global activism and community service, she believes that much lasting change in our world begins from the inside out. She is passionate about poetry, creative expression, aligning her activities with her interests, and helping others to similarly follow their bliss. Jeanine is currently exploring life's exciting terrain through her blog, Zest for the Quest. You can also follow her on Twitter @ZestForTheQuest.

Cassia Cogger is a mother and wife by sweet and sacred luck, an Internet expert by default, a former ironman by sweat and determination, a poet on purpose, and an artist by soul. She looks to catch stars wherever she goes. All of the above are totally related, and someday she might even tell us how. Until then, she's still figuring it all out. One of her tools for this self-exploration is writing.

Lauryn Doll is the sexy Digital Strategist behind Wild Topaz Media, which houses the Lauryn Doll, Sexy Focused Ambitious, and Beauty Sex Fitness brands. Lauryn began writing when she was in her late teens to vent frustrations after a very bad breakup and while going through general teen angst. Over time, her colorful way of saying things, coupled with her ability to ask the right questions, earned her a role as Associate Editor of J'ADORE Magazine.

Sang Thi Duong is a speaker, rock star scribe, and event social media commander. She is the founder of Sangtastik, where she canvasses the pavement in her Ferrari Red Heels and flowing satin scarf. Sang also teaches youth entrepreneurship and mentors teenage girls. When Sang is not networking, writing, or reading, she can be found taking time to breathe and living life while sipping on some Starbucks.

Jessica Glendinning is a seeker. A designer, writer, yogi, activist, and musician, passionate and a perfectionist, she adores alliteration and all things fuzzy. She grew up a weird kid, then lost herself somewhere along the way. Several years ago, she woke up, detached from society's expectations, and embraced her non-conformity. Her life is a constant evolution, a journey of discovery and improvement. She hopes to find herself somewhere along the way. Her one constant is this: she knows that she is here to save the world. She can be found online at VerdantSpringDesign.com.

Joshua Harbert helps people weave meaning and compassion into everyday moments. In 14 years growing up in Kenya, he witnessed the beauty and grace of humanity amid the injustices of poverty. Efforts to live, and help others live, into that humanity drive much of his thinking and writing. Specifically, he serves people on a mission by crafting action-generating copy and by sharing weekly stories/wisdom at The Bright Army. When he's not writing, you can find him wandering the neighborhoods of Chicago, training in Taekwondo, playing with his wife and daughter, or smiling at a squirrel.

Clare Herbert is a writer, career strategist, and social entrepreneur currently based in Dublin, Ireland. Her writing has been featured in a number of national publications including The Irish Times and The Sunday Times. As an entrepreneurial journalist, Clare has appeared on live national television and radio and has also spoken at a number of international conferences. Clare spent 10 years working in the non-profit sector across four continents, from Washington, D.C., to India to rural Zambia. Clare currently works as a career strategist supporting activists, change-makers, and social entrepreneurs, helping them build meaningful and impactful careers. Find her online at ClareHerbert.com.

Stephanie Jiroch is empowering women to live fun and fabulous lives by flirting with all that life has to offer. As the founder of Flirt With Life℠, Stephanie teaches women all over the world how to manifest their truest desires so they can start living their dream life without fear and with ease. She has spent the last six years working with women to enhance their lives physically, mentally, and emotionally as a coach, yoga instructor, and holistic health practitioner. Connect with her on Twitter @StephanieJiroch and visit StephanieJiroch.com for more ways to flirt with life.

Lisa Landtroop owns BXLNT (Be eXceLleNT), a multi-platform enterprise specializing in time awareness coaching, copywriting, editing, and proofing to encourage and support change leaders. She is the creator of the powerful course, Take Your Life Back, which helps changemakers remember that life is too short to do stuff you hate. Connect with Lisa on Twitter

@LisaLandtroop and reach her by email at Lisa@TQLTotalQualityLife.com.

Lori Mancini is a freelance television sports producer, yoga studio owner, and writer. Between her love of Boston sports, yoga, and communication, Lori believes in meeting passion, loyalty, and dedication in all areas of her life. Her yoga studio, Laughing Elephant Yoga, is based in East Greenwich, Rhode Island, and can be found at LaughingElephantYoga.com. When she's not working with major television networks like ESPN and CBS, she can be found biking across New England and walking her white Labrador retriever, Moses.

Milo McLaughlin is a former civil servant forging a new path in life as a content creator. He strongly believes that writers and other creative people can make a good living from work that is enjoyable and meaningful to them, but that it takes patience, determination, and a willingness to change limiting habits and beliefs. In 2011, Milo founded ClearMindedCreative.com to share his own journey and provide inspiration, support, and practical advice to other creative types in search of a more fulfilling life and career.

Tom Meitner is an author and copywriter living in Milwaukee, WI. After receiving his English degree and having zero direction in his life, he stumbled upon a book about freelance writing. Since then, he hasn't looked back, and has been happily freelancing and building businesses since the spring of 2008. You can usually find him hanging out at TomMeitner.com.

Amy Ouellette is an aspiring nutritarian, a retirement plan consultant, and a personal finance geek. She has been consulting and collecting credentials in the finance industry for almost 10 years, while student loans and other debt allowed her to turn her fear into a hunger for knowledge and action on the personal finance side. Amy's passion for writing is twofold: rediscovering journaling to explore her values and identity, and embracing those values as a means to help her connect with and teach others through story and inspiration. Find her on Twitter @aeouellette03.

Diane Pauley is a writer and life coach who has been writing since she was 6 years old. Diane carried her passion for the written word with her through high school, but abandoned her love of writing in pursuit of a "safe, money-making" career in law. Diane soon decided her heart wasn't in the traditional life-route, so she threw her safe plans out the window. Today, Diane has returned to her roots and is using her passion for people and written word to coach young post-grads who feel they've lost their way. Join Diane's mission to rediscover your true identity at PostGradolescence.com.

Jean Powell is the Director of Sales for Taphandles brewery marketing and is currently building a new beer branding agency. She believes sales to be the most powerful vehicle to grow personally and accelerate the development of those around her. Jean teaches the necessity and awesomeness of selling in everyday life, removing the fear and blocks from rejection and confrontation. Her desire is to revolutionize how managers lead teams, focusing on culture over strategy and heart over head. Jean is currently developing sales/sales management content and resources. Get updates and read more from her at JeanOnTap.com and on Twitter @JeanOnTap.

Jennifer Price is a copywriter who touches hearts and minds with words that give a graceful caress, a gentle nudge, and an oh-so-sweet feeling that inevitably leads to a "YES." She's a dreamteller who helps creative business owners express and realize their vision, bringing it to life with words. Jennifer's strong experience as a marketing and sales executive enables her to incite emotional response and allure loyal enthusiasts to unique brands. Jennifer is online at YouSoMuch.com.

Kadena Tate is a creative visionary and change agent who uses coaching, consulting, speaking, and training to help entrepreneurs leapfrog the market and make the competition irrelevant. A contributing author in the NYT Bestseller, Business Model You, she believes that authenticity has no competition. As a business acceleration alchemist, Kadena will help you gain the confidence and clarity necessary to attract clients, cash, and clout. Visit her online today at KadenaTate.com.

Dr. Rona Thau believes that life's most valuable asset is inner happiness, and has since her earliest memories. Rona has evolved as a spiritual creative, yogi, health doctor, and food lover, and is pioneering an Ageless Living Revolution as a way to connect people to inner happiness through food, movement, and mindset. Ageless Living lets you feel, function, and be free successfully. It's necessary now. We all deserve to be happy and free. As ageless living techniques catch on, the movement will be swift. It's a fun path. Connect with Rona at DrRonaThau.com.

Caitlin Walsh was born, raised, and currently lives in Boston, but took a four-year detour to Long Island for college. She dreams of being an author, of selling books in stores, and of earning a living by her printed words. For now, though, she works behind the scenes for a financial news website by day, and by night is usually knee deep in her novel draft or another writing project that she started to avoid her novel. She spends most of her free time on the T, traveling to various meet-ups, groups, and activities. She also lives on the Internet @WalshCaitlin.

Meagan Christine Williams is a writer, traveler, coach, and lover of people and the Universe. In August 2011, she was on track to become a part of the corporate world but realized something wasn't clicking. She longed for something more. So she quit business school to pursue her desire to change the world by helping people make their dreams come true and better their lives. Today, through writing and coaching, she helps others heal their hearts and discover the beauty and value within themselves while exploring her own passions: spirituality, creativity, love, and the Universe. She can be found at MeaganCWilliams.com.

Jason Vanfosson writes fiction and nonfiction. He is a life coach to artists, writers, creatives, and entrepreneurs who want to lead brazen lives of creativity. His alter ego is working on his Ph.D. in American literature at Western Michigan University, where he also teaches composition, introduction to literature, and American literature. You can read his super secret experimental blog and connect with him on social media by visiting JasonVanfosson.com.

Shine on.

www.ingramcontent.com/pod-product-compliance
Lightning Source LLC
Chambersburg PA
CBHW020916180526
45163CB00007B/2754